ARTHUR HUGH CLOUGH

Arthur Hugh Clough

JAMES INSLEY OSBORNE

OF PHILADELPHIA

PR
4458
O8
1920

105274

BOSTON AND NEW YORK
HOUGHTON MIFFLIN COMPANY
1920

CONTENTS

CHAPTER I

CHILDHOOD

ARTHUR HUGH CLOUGH was born in Liverpool on January 1, 1819. His father, James Butler Clough, was a cotton merchant, belonging to an old and respectable Welsh family. His mother's maiden name was Anne Perfect. She was the daughter of a banker living at Pontefract in Yorkshire.

There is little or nothing in the poet's ancestry to point to as indicative of forthcoming genius. From the days of Henry VIII the Cloughs had lived in the country, raised large families, and kept their annals brief. There was, indeed, an eighteenth-century Hugh Clough, friend of Cowper and Fellow of King's College, who got himself known as a poet ; but his example was hardly powerful enough to influence his younger kinsman. Were it not so remote, a reported relationship with John Calvin might furnish more interesting ground for speculation than this poetical connection.

The home county of the Cloughs was Denbighshire, in North Wales. There the foundations of a considerable family fortune had been laid by a sixteenth-century Sir Richard Clough, who invested in lands

7

and buildings in his native county the money he made in Antwerp as the agent of Sir Thomas Gresham, and in Hamburg as court master of the Fellowship of Merchant Adventurers. His descendants enjoyed considerable prosperity and respect throughout the following two centuries without finding it necessary to bestir themselves particularly. But one Roger Clough of the late eighteenth century, a clergyman and the grandfather of Arthur Hugh, lost in a bank failure the greater part both of his own fortune and the fortune he had married, and left his ten children comparatively impoverished. James Butler was the third child. He left Wales to go into business in Liverpool, married there in 1816, and had four children—Charles Butler, born 1817; Arthur Hugh, 1819; Anne Jemima, 1820; and George Augustus, 1821.

Arthur Clough and his sister both mention their mother's family, the Perfects, only in connection with a specific family imperfection. Arthur alludes to it in a letter he writes from Rugby to his younger brother : "Only remember, don't be indolent, George ; you recollect what I told you about that family failing. Idle, I do not think you will be ; but take care you never say, ' It is too much trouble,' ' I can't be bothered,' which are tolerably old favourites of yours, and indeed of all who have any Perfect blood in them." Whatever trouble it may have given his brother, the family failing did not prevent Arthur Hugh's life from becoming a record of close application to duty. Or it affected him perhaps, from this point of view, in the manner of an inoculation, somewhat as the shiftlessness of the elder Dickens was a principal cause of the amazing industry of his son. But it is possible to view the poet's life in another light, in which his freedom from Perfect indolence is not so certain. Perhaps he seemed busier than, in a narrower sense, he really was. After all, he regarded writing as his work, and yet wrote little. His other activities, so vigorously pursued, would appear in this light as evasions rather than efforts, as devices for distracting the attention from the one point to which a more genuine industry would have kept it turned.

This appearance of a certain mental laziness in Clough's adult life has been connected, very much less reasonably, with another circumstance—the fact that as a child he lived in a warm climate. Late in the year 1823 the Cloughs removed from Liverpool to Charleston, South Carolina, which was their home for some thirteen years. Arthur returned to England in 1828 to enter school. He was in Charleston therefore from his fourth to his tenth year. The summers during this period were spent by the Cloughs either in the North, or, very pleasantly, we are told, on Sullivan's Island out in the bay. Under these conditions the Charleston climate would have to be very hot indeed to explain much in the poet's matured character.

For the *Memoir* prefixed to the 1869 edition of the Poems, Anne Jemima Clough supplied some recollections of this period of her brother's life. This is the Miss Clough who became, in 1871, the first Principal of Newnham College, Cambridge. The family lived at Charleston, she says, in " a large, ugly, red-brick house " on the East Bay. The father had his office on the ground floor of the building. His visitors were planters from the river and captains of sailing vessels, and his premises were piled with bagging and twine and cotton. From their nursery windows the children could watch the ships standing at the wharves, and passing in and out of the bay. They would have had to be very prosaic children not to find their surroundings rich in the materials of wonder and make-believe. It is a little singular that the one of them presumably the most sensitive, the poet to be, never voiced, in his later writings, any recollection of these unusual scenes of his childhood.

But the Cloughs " were very English," as one of their descendants remarks, and especially English in the first five years of their stay in South Carolina, the years before the two elder boys went back to England to school. They did not allow their children to go to any of the local schools, nor help them to make friends with the American children. Mrs. Clough made no effort to become acquainted with the people of the city. She reminded her son continually that he was a Briton ; toward

American traditions she created in her home an attitude of indifference rather than of sympathy or active hostility, either of which would have stimulated a small boy's curiosity concerning the picturesque scenes and people about him. Being very loyal to his mother, and very receptive to her suggestions, Arthur stayed in her room and read about English sea captains of the past, instead of lingering about his father's office to admire living American sea captains. And so—to speak in a dangerously serious way of the responsibilities of a child—missing the romance and the humour that were close about him in this first environment he confronted, this child established a fair likelihood that if he ever became a poet, his poetry would be chiefly remarkable for other riches than romance or humour.

Arthur Clough at seven, in his sister's account, is "a beautiful boy, with soft, silky, almost black hair, and shining dark eyes, and a small delicate mouth." He reads a great deal, is passionate, but obstinate rather than easily roused, and is too fastidious to go barefooted. He studies history and books of travel with his mother, and is accustomed to "do sums in the office, lying on the piled-up pieces of cotton bagging."

During these years the father was frequently away on business, and Arthur, his sister tells, came to be his mother's constant companion. "She poured out the fullness of her heart on him." Her influence on him was great. She was very religious, and spoke to her children early and late about God and about Duty. She strove to inculcate in them her own enthusiasm for all that was noble and other-worldly. Her attachments were few and of great strength. She was very affectionate, and clinging, and womanly. Her influence, in short, was of precisely the sort to make a conscientious and idealistic boy quite *too* conscientious and idealistic. The really remarkable thing about this influence was that it was direct and positive. Many a similarly pious nineteenth century mother succeeded in implanting in the breast of a similarly sensitive son a fierce ambition to become as hard as nails. The difference in the case of Mrs. Clough and her son was mainly that she had him to herself, without much interference from his father, or from relatives and friends ; but partly too, perhaps, that the attraction between them was especially strong. One result of all this was that when the family went to visit its cousins, on its return to England, Arthur, in the words of his sister, " could not enter into the boys' rough games and amusements." It is a frequent circumstance in the childhood of poets, so frequent that to regret it would almost be to regret poets.

Clough's father seems to have been a cheerful and active, though not uniformly successful, business man, very affectionate toward his family, with a lively interest in the surface of things, and no interest at all in what lay beneath the surface. He cared much for company and little for books. He had great zest for doing things and for moving about. His inclinations in these matters were quite the opposite of his wife's. And though it was the mother's tendency that relatives and friends were accustomed to find dominant in Arthur, they found something of his father in him also. A zest for doing things was certainly characteristic of Clough the schoolboy, though it was to disappear from Clough the undergraduate. His sister felt that in his later years he came to resemble their father very decidedly. His liking for the passing show, his tact, and his constant watchfulness for the comfort of those about him, are qualities she ascribes to the paternal influence. But whatever may be true of the adult Clough, the small boy was certainly his mother's son much more than his father's. This is true, doubtless, of most boys. But it was exceptionally true of Clough.

In June 1828 the Cloughs made a journey to England. When the rest of the family returned to America in October, they left Arthur and his elder brother, Charles, in a school in Chester. Here they remained until the summer of the next year, when they both entered Rugby. A letter written by Arthur to his sister from the Chester school attests the association in the youthful mind of a pictorial talent and a taste for sensation with a breadth of interest truly Baconian. "During the Easter holidays," it runs, "I had plenty of leisure for drawing. Two men were hung here lately for robbing an old clergyman. We have bought a book entitled *The New-tonian System of Philosophy*, which treats chiefly of the power and weight of air ; the cause of volcanoes, earthquakes, and other phenomena of nature, such as lightning, the aurora borealis ; also a description of the sun, planets, their moons or satellites, constellations, comets, and other heavenly bodies ; likewise of air-guns, balloons, air-pumps ; also a very pleasing one of snow, hail, and vapours. It also describes electricity and magnetism, and gives a brief account of minerals, vegetables, and animals." How much the account of the book sounds as if Bacon himself were describing a notable publication of his House of Saloman ! And sounding like the sagest science of an earlier age, how childish, too, it sounds ! Here is the gust of childhood for the last time in anything we have of Clough's until *The Bothie*, written in the zest of holiday release from academic walls, twenty years later. For in the eleventh year of his childhood, Clough was turned over to Arnold of Rugby, to be kindly and firmly and prematurely inducted into manhood.

CHAPTER II

AT RUGBY

WHEN the Clough boys were entered at Rugby, Dr. Arnold had been there only a year, and had just begun the work of his reform. It has always been agreed that this reform wrought a transformation in English public life. It is not so clearly appreciated that the actual changes in school organization and curriculum which it involved were few and slight. An increase of pay for assistant masters, with a corresponding increase in school fees, a little more of modern history and English literature in the course of study, the recognition of the old fagging system as a regular means of discipline—these were the main, and almost the only, changes in the outer constitution of the school. The great change was a change of spirit. Arnold insisted before anything else on building character into his charges. Boys will be boys, had been the reflection of previous schoolmasters ; but Arnold remembered that boys would be men. The old rules and the old punishments were perfunctory ; they rested on a dim feeling that restrictions and beatings were a wholesome element in boy routine. Arnold punished severely if he punished at all, and always with a clear view of some benefit to be secured. He resolutely expelled boys of whose moral influence he was dubious. Those that stayed he laboured to place beyond the necessity of punishment, by forcing the growth in them of conscience and self-control.

It was a task of leadership more than of command which Arnold had set himself, and he brought genius to the performance of it. He really succeeded in breaking down the long-standing hostility between boys and masters. He really brought his boys to the point of imitating his own character and conduct, and even to the farther point of thinking as he did about the duties and opportunities of the school.

Arthur Clough went to Rugby, his sister writes, "a somewhat grave and studious boy, not without tastes for walking, shooting, and sight-seeing, but with little capacity for play and for mixing with others." Life in the school made up the first, and in great part the second, of these deficiencies. Clough acquired skill at the Rugby games, and he made friends. In athletics his record is not merely of the kind so frequently pieced out for boys who are really not so titanic or so agile as they might have been. No less thoroughly competent an authority than the author of *Tom Brown's Schooldays* asserts that at the queen of the Rugby games Clough was the best goal-keeper of his day ; but he adds that, though he swam well too, Clough did not take a prominent part in games. Other authorities are less inclined to minimize Clough's prowess. William D. Arnold, for instance, in a pamphlet, of interest to Rugbeians, called *Football : the Sixth Match*, says something of the work of the forward and centre positions in the game, and then : " Lastly there are those who feel that keeping goal, defending the very crown of conquest, is no mean or unworthy task, since beneath those very bars were given to immortality the names of Clough and Harry Thorpe." Clough's name stands on the athletic roll of honour in the further capacity of first recorded winner of the " Barbey Hill Run," the oldest of the official runs of the school. But of course the games of Rugby and the winners in them were numerous. Clough's accomplishment at sports, it may be concluded, was up to the average, and not above it.

Clough's friends at Rugby were nearly all men who later went into the Church, and attained more or less prominence as upholders of latitudinarian ideas. One who looks through the Rugby roll of the years of Arnold's mastership is struck by the fact that it divides itself almost half and half into soldiers and clergymen. The other callings are but thinly represented. Of the soldiers there are not a few that made themselves famous in the Crimean War. Not one of them is represented as a correspondent or even by mention in the volume of Clough's letters. They, presumably, were the less sensitive members of the school, who indeed also received Arnold's inspiration toward devotion to duty, but only in such measure as left unimpaired the vigorous life of instinct and of impulse. These constituted Clough's opportunities for forming friendships outside the limits of the one way of taking life in which he had been brought up. And he failed to avail himself of them.

Of the men older than himself that he knew well the strongest personalities were presumably three men who were later to become deans of cathedrals. Arthur P. Stanley, though he entered Rugby six months later than Clough, was his senior by three years. In later years both the poet and the Dean of Westminster testified to a high mutual esteem ; in schooldays the admiration must have been mainly on the side of Clough. That the two made much the same kind of impression on their schoolmates appears from the circumstance that while the boy Arthur in *Tom Brown's Schooldays* has generally been taken as a portrait of Stanley, a number of contemporary Rugbeians thought that Clough was the author's model. Still other " Arthurs," except in name, must C. J. Vaughan and W. C. Lake have been, lifelong disciples of Arnold both, Vaughan as Headmaster of Harrow, Master of the Temple, and Dean of Llandaff, successively, and Lake as Dean of Durham. Boys of less brilliant futures, but doubtless equal purity of character, and dear friends of Clough, were Thomas Burbidge, J. P. Gell, and J. N. Simpkinson. Burbidge went to Aberdeen University and then to

Cambridge, was Master of Leamington College for
a time, and then for many years a chaplain of English congregations in the cities of the Mediterranean.
It was with him that Clough joined in the publication of *Ambarvalia*, in 1848. Gell and Simpkinson
became Trinity men at Cambridge, taught for a time,
Gell in Tasmania and Simpkinson at Harrow, and
concluded their lives as rectors of churches respec-
tively in London and in the country. Of younger
friends the most noteworthy are the Arnold boys,
Matthew and Thomas. They entered their father's
school only in the summer preceding Clough's last
year of residence, but he had known them well before
that time while they were living at home, and
during vacations from their earlier schooling at
Winchester. With the Arnold boys is associated
Theodore Walrond, an attractive boy from the
North, well-loved though not fated to accomplish
any memorable work in the world.

This, practically, is the list of Clough's intimate
companions at school. It is remarkable for the
brilliancy it comprises, but still more remarkable
for its homogeneity. To at least three of the number
has been applied the epithet "Doctor Arnold's
favourite pupil." They were all boys after his heart
—boys also of just the kind Mrs. Clough would have
chosen as associates for her son.

In addition to his intimates Clough had a great
number of admiring acquaintances. We are told
that he was the most prominent boy in the school in

his last year, and that when he left nearly every boy in Rugby shook him by the hand. In the light of a letter which he wrote in the next to the last year of his residence, it is perhaps not wholly cynical to suggest that this ovation awarded to his departure may have rested on some confusion of motives. He complains in this letter that he is " of necessity thrown much with other fellows, and wishing now most earnestly to know as many as possible ; for there is a deal of evil springing up in the school, and it is to be feared that the tares will choke much of the wheat." It is conceivable that many a palpable tare was amiable on the occasion of Clough's leaving from a feeling that saying farewell to him was not after all immeasurably less satisfactory than choking him would have been.

For it was undoubtedly possible, then as now, to look upon the schoolboy Clough as a prig. He was saved from the more serious degrees of priggishness by the honesty and wholeheartedness and unselfishness with which he plunged into the life of the school. He played his games with a little more of Dr. Arnold's own consciousness of the moral value of athletic exercises than comports with the ideal of care-free, joyous youth ; yet he played them zealously and well.

He had a stronger and more spontaneous interest in his studies, and was remarkably successful in them. Before he was fourteen he won the only scholarship the school afforded. He progressed rapidly through the forms, until he had to wait a year to get into the sixth, because he was under the age limit for it.   In his various classes he was winning prizes continually : in a single letter to his mother he is likely to mention as many as five or six new ones. Toward the end of his next to last year he writes her : " As for the prizes, I have this Easter got one, the Latin verse ; and a second for each of the others, viz. the Latin prose and the Greek verse, so that I shall still have two to try for next year ; so that, of course, I am very well satisfied."   In pursuits corresponding to our " student activities " of to-day, he was equally successful.   He held what administrative offices there were, and was editor and chief contributor of the *Rugby Magazine*.

But the most significant thing about Rugby life for Clough was that it provided such a perfect hotbed for fostering the preoccupation with morality and religion implanted in him by his mother.   Here as at home he lived under constant incitement to emulate the loftiest models of Christian conduct. The atmosphere of the school differed from that of the home chiefly, perhaps, in that it inculcated a responsibility for the actions of others than oneself.   Because he was early singled out as desirable material for leadership, Clough was particularly encouraged by Dr. Arnold to assume an intense feeling of accountability for the morals of the entire school.   He was Arnold's favourite as distinctly as he had been his mother's favourite.   Matthew Arnold's elder brother

Thomas writes that Clough spent much of his time in the private part of the master's house. He was made especially welcome there " by his gentleness and sincerity." He was thus exposed more completely even than Arnold's own partly Wykehamist sons, to the powerful personal influence of a man whose chief defect as a schoolmaster was that he failed to appreciate the utterly different effects his system would have on the ordinary " roundabout boy," and on a boy like Clough—or else that he really believed such a morally over-trained product as Clough was when he left for Oxford was the proper end of public-school training.

The schoolboy letters of Clough that have been preserved were nearly all written in the last two years of his residence ; and they show clearly that at any rate in that final period he considered himself as on the side rather of the masters than of the pupils. He is continually writing to his friends sentiments that would be unendurably priggish if they were not so admirably and pathetically sincere—such things as this : " I verily believe my whole being is soaked through with the wishing and hoping and striving to do the school good, or rather to keep it up and hinder it from falling in this, I do think, very critical time, so that all my cares and affections and conversations, thoughts, words, and deeds, look to that involuntarily."

The crisis Clough refers to is apparently the Tory attack on the Broad Church principles, on the peculiarly effective discipline, and on what was taken to be the goody-goodiness of Rugby. For a time the weight of this attack was shown in a decided falling off in attendance. The situation may well have seemed critical to those who believed that the fate of a reform very badly needed not only by Rugby but by all the English public schools was hanging in the balance. Fate decided, of course, in favour of Arnold. The superiority of the clean-living and industrious Rugbeian to the slack and irreverent product of the other schools became very obvious when they met together as freshmen at the Universities. Among the rivals and opponents of Dr. Arnold who recognized the excellence of the men he made is Cardinal Newman, who says, in the *Apologia*, of the Broad Church movement : " The party grew all the time that I was in Oxford, even in numbers, certainly in breadth and definiteness of doctrine, and in power. And, what was a far higher consideration, by the accession of Dr. Arnold's pupils, it was invested with an elevation of character which claimed the respect even of its opponents." Such men as Vaughan and Stanley and Lake, with others as substantial if less distinguished, were a sufficient answer to the charges levied against the system that produced them ; and within a few years the important elements of the Rugby system were in highly advantageous operation in Eton and Harrow and Westminster and Winchester.

It was a really great reform, and Clough, young as

he was, seems to have been fully aware of its significance. And to him must go at least so much credit
for the result as belongs to the best of a small set of
highly efficient tools. It was in his favour that Dr.
Arnold broke his rule of delivering prizes with no
comment, congratulating him publicly on having
won every Rugby honour, and on having served his
school well. In him Dr. Arnold found a servant
ready to subject his own will completely, able to
win the leadership of the school, and desirous of
using that leadership to no other end than the fur-
therance of his master's purposes. To keep up a
favourable spirit in the school was, of course, the
very essence of Dr. Arnold's success. It is almost
possible to suspect that a little of the spirit of rebellion in Clough might have sealed the doom of the
Rugby experiment. However disastrous this dash
of rebelliousness might have been to the course of
education and morality in England, it would, perhaps, have been an excellent thing in the long run
for the happiness, the individuality, and the poetical
quality of Clough.

Assuming that Clough was destined from the first
to become a poet, and a moral poet, it might be
supposed that the strong and delightful moral atmosphere of Rugby was peculiarly favourable to his
poetical development. But it is a principle of re-
pulsion that operates in such cases more frequently
than a principle of attraction. A sensitive youth is
more likely to be driven into poetry by uncongenial,

than led into it by congenial, circumstances. When
he can see his ideals being actively striven after
by his community he is likely to join in the struggle
rather than to stand off and meditate those ideals
and vent in mere song the emotions to which they
give rise. When his outer life is such that the boy's
heart can be in it, the demand of his inner life for
expression, for lyrical outpouring, will probably
not be insistent, nor even genuine.

Clough's life at Rugby is a splendid record of
youthful steadiness and purpose and energy, but it
is a better explanation how to hinder than how to
promote the education of a poet. He was in com-
pletest measure the prize schoolboy ; but he is alone
among English poets in having enjoyed that distinction. For the development even of the classical
poet, the Pope or the Johnson, some principle of
isolation is necessary, some occasion for the awakening of individual perceptions and ideas distinct from
the ideas and perceptions of the community. There
is not much detachment in the usual boy's life, but
detachment is essential to the life of the boy who is
to be a poet. A number of Clough's contemporaries
considered that his adolescence was greatly prolonged
—or better, long interrupted. He was more a boy
when he left than when he entered Oxford. And
it was at Oxford that he learned to separate himself from those about him. But at Rugby he
was interested in the community life to the point
of being completely fused in it. His loyalty to the

school was complete ; and everything he did and said was an expression, not properly of himself, but of this loyalty.

His school-life was remarkable in precisely contrary respects to those in which we are accustomed to find the school-lives of poets remarkable. It was not rebellious, we have said, like Shelley's or Byron's ; nor shrinking and self-contained, like Coleridge's ; nor lighted up by enthusiasm for poetry, like Keats's ; nor largely taken up with day-dreaming, like the life of almost any other poet than himself that might be named.

With most young poets, reading at sweet will has been the main road to the detachment necessary to the artist. But there is nothing to show that Clough found much time out of school hours for browsing in a library. The only publications mentioned in the letters from Rugby, the reading of which cannot be taken to have been obligatory, are three newspapers and *Knight's Quarterly*. Perhaps Clough read more during his earlier, less responsible years at school. His sister speaks of his rushing to show his mother the delightful discovery he had made of Johnson's *Lives of the Poets*. This was in 1831, when he was still in the period of his childhood enjoyment of Scott and Robertson and Pope's Homer. Later his love of reading seems to have vanished along with his other impulses under the shadow of his all-subduing sense of duty.

One kind of detachment Clough attained at

Rugby, and that is moral detachment. Milton's
youth proves that it is possible to combine this
detachment of the moralist with the detachment
that springs from a keen perception of beauty.
But in Milton's youth beauty came first, which is
as it should be in the youth of a poet, but is not
as it was in the youth of Clough. Wordsworth
too effected a reconciliation of the two things ;
but Wordsworth had the useful conviction that he
could best learn morality from the trees, which are
very beautiful, whereas Clough was persuaded that
he could best learn morality from Dr. Arnold, who
unfortunately was not nearly so beautiful as he was
good. With the young Wordsworth and the young
Milton morality was a matter more of reflection than
of getting things done—and reflection shades off
easily and naturally into imagination. But not so,
getting things done. Give a strong sense of duty,
many things to do, and the exercise of the imagination becomes at once a wasteful sin. This is just
what happened in the case of the Rugbeian Clough :
he was robbed of all opportunity for building his
castles in Spain, for creating for himself

> "Such sights as youthful Poets dream
> On summer eves by haunted stream."

He literally had no time for the " wish-thinking "
which modern psychology says is the making of the
painter, the musician, and the poet. The country
about Rugby, though not so beautiful as that
about Horton or Grasmere, is yet much the same

country as that about Stratford-on-Avon ; but Clough had no time to look at it. There was beauty in the high spirits of wayward Rugby boys ; but Clough was set at looking out vigilantly for every least appearance of evil in this quarter. His vacations afforded beautiful cousins as well as beautiful scenes, and stirred in him strange emotions. But so far were these emotions from having the right of way in his life, that they were only made serviceable for beauty, taken up as themes for poetry, when they had been mellowed by the passage of twenty-five years.

Almost as striking as the absence from the Rugby letters of a concern about beauty, is the absence of any sign of wit or humour. There is only one slip in the direction of pleasantry, and that is immediately exposed to publicity and apologized for. This is the line : " The kind of passive and almost apathetic feeling (to indulge in a bull)——" This is the nearest approach to a joke.

Also notable is the absence of any mark of interest in the doings of the outside world. Clough's thoughts fly half-way over the Rugby walls in connection with the ecclesiastical and educational controversies of Dr. Arnold ; and he is interested toward the last in Oxford and Cambridge as rival entertainers of Rugby men. When men at the universities come back to visit, he is attracted not by their travellers' tales but by their comments on the school. " It is very fine and striking," he says, " to see many of the best and cleverest Oxford and Cambridge men still watching with great interest all the little changes in the school, and still helping those that remain with their experience and wisdom." And when the time finally comes for his own departure, he is only consoled by the reflection, " that Dr. Arnold will be a bishop before long."

The experience, then, which Clough spent the most susceptible years of his life in storing up, was mainly of one sole kind, not of many kinds. At the time when it was most natural and most important for his mind to be wide open, he kept it three-quarters closed—or if conduct really is three-fourths of life, then one-quarter closed. He learned too early, for artistic purposes, to regulate and analyse his thoughts. In part deliberately and in part through preoccupation he limited narrowly the range of his curiosity in people and things. So doing made it very difficult for him ever to come to really close grips with certain large classes of thoughts and desires. Against the ravages of later introspection he stored the larder with far too limited a range of foods. Connections which youthful intuition might have taken in at a glance, if given the opportunity, he was later compelled to puzzle out at vast expense of middle-age reasoning. The sympathies of his adult years, wide as earth in the number of persons they touched, were yet narrow in that they touched most of those persons only at one or two points. A rather bitter awareness of this limitation is

back of the lines in the Second Part of *Dipsychus*,
in which the retiring Chief Justice is described
by one of the barristers :

> " He was a moral sort of prig, I've heard,
>   Till he was twenty-five ; and even then
>   He never entered into life as most men.
>   That is the reason why he fails so soon."

Considerably more natural and youthful seem to
have been Clough's activities in his vacations.
Except for the summer of 1833, and his last year,
he was separated from his family during his schooldays by the width of the Atlantic.   But he had many
relatives in England and in Wales, and he visited
about among these, very welcome, it appears, and
for the most part very happy.   In the last year
of his life, he turned back to this part of his experience for the subject matter of " Primitiae," the best of
the tales in *Mari Magno*.   It is a happy little story
in the main, but with a rather pathetic reminis-
cence of upper-form preoccupation with books
and problems breaking in destructively on the easy
and affectionate relations previously established
with charming young cousins.   It is pretty certainly
to these vacations that Clough owes the first springing in him of a more humorous and critical and
worldly self.   This summer Clough was in complete
subjection through school and college to the Rugbeian
winter Clough, and indeed never completely
triumphed over him, effecting at best an equal
partnership, if not a fusion, in the poet's last years.

In 1836 the Clough family moved from Charleston back to Liverpool. Arthur Hugh with fervid eloquence poured out before his parents the liberal ideas he had been imbibing from Dr. Arnold. And they, being Tories, regretted at times that they had not sent their son to Shrewsbury. But they were proud of him, and vastly content with his Rugby successes. His sister renewed at this time the love for him, amounting to veneration, that was the great emotional experience of her long and useful life. He was almost equally fond of her, and delighted in sharing his enthusiasms with her, and inspiring her with his own and Dr. Arnold's great ambition to do good work in the world.

What has previously been said about the schoolboy Clough's lack of the earmarks of the artist takes no account of the undisputed fact that he wrote while he was at Rugby a certain quantity of verse. The *Memoir* states that in his first year at school " he was perpetually writing verses, not remarkable except for a certain ease of expression and for a power of running on, not common at that early age." Cares of a scholarly and of a pastoral kind seem to have obstructed the progress of the muse in the higher forms. At any rate only two or three schoolboy poems are published along with the later productions. Of these the one called " An Incident " is a direct imitation of Wordsworth, the Wordsworth of " We are Seven." It is very moral, very carefully simple, and rather pretty. " An Evening Walk in

Spring " is more interesting. It is very Words-
worthian too, and very sentimental, but it is obviously the result of a real emotional experience. The
young poet finds himself unprevented by a scene of
peace and quiet joy from sinking into a conviction
of guilt. This conviction, characteristically enough,
remains unweakened by the failure of a diligent
search for some empirical evidence to explain it.
Then the thought comes of a sick friend (one of the
Arnold boys), and the depressing beauties of nature
are quickly left behind for the more appealing atmosphere of the sick-room. If, as seems likely, the
lesson of the poem is to be found in the lines :

> " And then there came the thought of one
> Who on his bed of sickness lay,
> Whilst I beneath the setting sun
> Was dreaming this sweet hour away "—

if the lesson is here, that lesson is the precarious one
for a boy wanting to become a poet, that it is very
wrong to dream sweet hours away. True, the lesson
once taken to heart, the loveliness of the scene is
no longer wasted on the boy, and brings tears of
joy to his eyes as he turns them away from it. But
the emphasis of the piece is all on inward beauty ;
any scene, we may suppose, will be beautiful when
looked at from eyes glowing with the right intensity
of goodness.

It was perhaps the foremost quality of the adult
Clough that he was a quite exceptionally perceptive
and honest critic of his own nature, his own philo-

sophy, and his own life. He has provided us with
some comment on his experience at Rugby, which
goes beyond other criticism of the effect of the school
on him in pronouncing that effect deleterious. He
writes this criticism in the *Epilogue to Dipsychus*.
Most of it is put into the mouth of the uncle that the
poet provides for himself as hero. Much of it—it
is not long, of course—has more important bearing
on later stages of Clough's life, and will be considered
in later chapters. But a few lines must be quoted
here. The uncle gets to the subject through some
talk about tender consciences : these are all too
common, he says : " schoolboy consciences, too !
As my old friend the Canon says of the Westminster
students, ' They're all so pious.' It's all Arnold's
doing ; he spoilt the public school." The poet, of
course, represents himself as protesting against this
extreme conclusion. His relative upholds the old
schools, claiming for them, not perfection, but that
" whatever else they were or did, they certainly were
in harmony with the world, and they certainly did
not disqualify the country's youth for after-life and
the country's service." His nephews, reared on the
Arnold plan, seem to this worthy English gentleman
" a sort of hobbledehoy cherub, too big to be inno-
cent, and too simple for anything else. They're full
of the notion of the world being so wicked and of
their taking a higher line, as they call it. I only
fear they'll never take any line at all. What is the
true purpose of education ? Simply to make plain to

c

the young understanding laws of the life they will have to enter. For example—that lying won't do, thieving still less ; that idleness will get punished ; that if they are cowards the whole world will be against them ; that if they will have their own way they must fight for it. As for the conscience— mamma, I take it,—such as mammas are nowadays, at any rate—has probably set that agoing fast enough already."

Another avuncular speech brings the question down directly to the case of the poet : " Put him " (the schoolboy) " through a strong course of confirm- ation and sacraments, backed up with sermons and private admonitions, and what is much the same as auricular confession, and really, my dear nephew, I can't answer for it but he mayn't turn out as great a goose as you—pardon me—*were* about the age of eighteen or nineteen."

This is extreme criticism, and it is not necessary, nor admissible, to take it as a careful statement of Clough's own views. It is a statement, rather, of one of two opposing opinions concerning the value of his training for life between which, as between two opinions of the value of life itself, the Clough of Dipsychus was wavering. Assuming as a third, and in some sort final and real, opinion the mean between these two contrary views, we may take it, perhaps, that if Clough still thought Rugby had done him good, he thought also that Rugby had done him harm. It had taught him much, but it had concealed much.

Its philosophy, in the pure and unalloyed form in which he had adopted it, had started him on a path that was removed from the highroad of life, and had stood in his way when the desire grew upon him to leave the path for the road.

Clough had unusually firm friends all his life, but there was a completeness about his personal ascendancy at Rugby which he never again approached. In the school he went about proselytizing, very genuinely for the good of the proselytes and not for any selfish purpose ; but in later life he had always too strong a sense that his own position might shift, or was shifting, to desire to call recruits to his banner. He had at Rugby the strength that comes from singleness of mind. His life to the time that he left for Oxford is a record of uninterrupted pursuit of a certain very definite and limited set of ideals. He devoted his every energy and ardour to these ideals. Naturally he attained great successes and profound respect. It is conceivable that he might have retained to the end this arrow straightness of direction and arrow swiftness of speed. The difficulty was that the Arnold spirit, like many another theme of eloquence and of jest, bore within itself the seeds of its own destruction. It insisted, that is, first of all, on looking everything straight in the face. A few of the things which presented themselves for Clough to look at when he found himself outside Rugby were Newmanism, scepticism, and utilitarianism ; and he soon discovered that a first necessity of looking all three of these variously placed monsters straight in the face at the same time, was totally incompatible with rapid progress in any single direction.

On the basis mainly of examination, Clough won in his last year at school a scholarship in Balliol College, the highest honour to which an English schoolboy could attain. Everybody who knew him quite confidently and interestedly expected that he would win all the prizes of Oxford as he had won all the prizes of Rugby. He himself doubtless shared in that opinion at first, but rather taking it as a matter of course, apparently, than feeling at all excited about it.

Clough spent with his family the summer after he finished this work at Rugby, and went up to Oxford University in October 1837.

CHAPTER III

AS UNDERGRADUATE

IN Oxford Clough was to spend eleven years—
four as an undergraduate, at Balliol, an inter-
mediate year of orientation, and six years as fellow
of Oriel. In his own life this was the period from his
nineteenth to his thirtieth year. In the life of the
University these were the years of the growth, the
maturity, and the fall of the Oxford Movement.
The propaganda had started in 1833. When Clough
came up to his college four years later it was in full
career. It continued for four years more to make
progress. Tract Ninety came out in 1841, calling
into ferocious activity all the hostility to itself
that the Movement had contracted. Four years of
tension and anxiety followed. Newman joined the
Church of Rome in 1845 ; and the University was
occupied during the last three years of Clough's
residence, and for a much longer time than that, in
the attempt to repair the damage and to secure the
good that the Movement had done to the Established
Church.

So important was the Movement, in Oxford
eyes, so admirable its leaders—or their rivals—so
exciting its controversies, so grave its issues, that
it attracted to itself nearly all the free intellectual
activity of the University. Politics the Tractarians

turned over to the impossible Liberals, pending
the time when an invincible weapon against them
should be available in a thoroughly reorganized,
mediaevalized Church. Literature was given up
to the mercies of the plebeian Dickens, the philistine
Macaulay, and that unaccountable stranger, Carlyle.
Science was left to confer upon London University
the unenvied title of Stinkomalee. Oxford talked,
and thought, and dreamed Religion.

Much of this preoccupation with religious questions
is to be explained by the essentially ecclesiastical
character of the University rather than by the attraction of a particular movement. Oxford was much
more of a Church institution in the first half of the
nineteenth century than it is now. Signing the
Articles was a necessary step not only in gaining
admittance to the University in the first place, but
also in accepting any college fellowship or tutorship.
Nearly all the "dons" were celibate, many of
them priests or deacons in the Church. After
scholarship, or in many cases before scholarship,
religion was their business. As their part in the
change in all fields of effort from the dullness and
neglect of the eighteenth century to the anxious
activity of the nineteenth, it was the task of the
senior members of the University to speed up religion
no less than to speed up learning. Something had
to be done to strengthen the Church, on the one hand
against nonconformity, and on the other against
the rapidly quickening interest in affairs purely of

this world. Before the Oxford Movement started Whately and Arnold, among others, had set about reforming, but in a Latitudinarian, not in the Roman, direction. In other words, a movement more or less like the Tractarian Movement was natural and necessary in the 'thirties and 'forties at Oxford. It is only the particular form that this tendency was to take which was decided by the conjunction of those three remarkable characters, Keble and Newman and Hurrell Froude.

These three men were young, as it is natural that reformers should be. They were young in years when they started their work, and they were careful to retain their youthful simplicity of spirit and accessibility. They made a great point of exerting the greatest possible personal influence on the minds of undergraduates. Newman in his *Apologia*, though he remarks in one place, " To the last I never recognized the hold I had over young men," says in another place, " It was through friends, younger for the most part than myself, that my principles were spreading. They heard what I said in conversation, and told it to others. Undergraduates in due time took their degree, and became private tutors themselves. In this new status they in turn preached the opinions with which they had already become acquainted." So there was built up and kept in operation a regular system of leadership by tutors of undergraduate opinion. An undergraduate might make of himself a social leader or an athletic leader, a man like Drysdale of *Tom Brown at Oxford*, or a man like Hardy, but he could hardly hope to become a leader by virtue of his intellectual force or his religious earnestness.

This was particularly true of Oxford at the time of the all-absorbing Movement ; but it is always true of a university, to an extent at least in which it is not true of a secondary school. The master of a great school, Arnold at Rugby for instance, is so far over the heads of his young pupils, his stature so great in comparison with theirs, that he can exercise an effective leadership, not directly, but only indirectly through trustworthy and advanced boys of the upper grades of the school. To a boy of this sort power comes down from above as if through an electrical transformer, and in the proud excitement of early responsibility he forgets the derived nature of it, and builds up in himself such a feeling of personal authority as hinders him ever thereafter from easily and naturally becoming a follower of any other man. He has over-developed his will and his thinking powers, just as another man has over-developed in athletics the muscles of his heart. And just as there is danger to the athlete in a too sudden letting down from habits of strenuous exercise, so there are serious possibilities of loss of tone in the young leader who finds himself suddenly left with nobody to lead.

It was an experience of this sort which Clough passed through in proceeding from Rugby to Oxford, and which may perhaps be taken to account for the unexpectedly poor showing that he made at the University. At Rugby he carried off all the prizes and distinctions available ; at Oxford he won few prizes, if any, and finished his undergraduate career by becoming the first Balliol scholar since the beginning of class lists to fall down to a second in the schools. It is usual to account for this slowing up in Clough by the assertion that in coming under the influence first of Arnold and then of Newman he was subjected to a strain that was both too long continued and too much the same thing from first to last. For instance, one of his best friends at Balliol, Mr. W. G. Ward, a Tractarian who later followed Newman into the Church of Rome, said of Clough : " What was before all things to have been desired for him, was that during his undergraduate career he should have given himself up thoroughly to his classical and mathematical studies, and kept himself from plunging prematurely into the theological controversies then so rife at Oxford. Thus he would have been saved from all injury to the gradual and healthy growth of his mind and character. It is my own very strong impression that, had this been permitted, his future course of thought and speculation would have been essentially different from what it was in fact. Drawn as it were peremptorily, when a young man just coming up to college, into a decision upon questions the most important that can occupy the mind, the result was not surprising. After this premature forcing of Clough's mind, there came a reaction. His intellectual perplexity preyed heavily on his spirits, and grievously interfered with his studies."

Ward knew Clough well, but his own absorption in religious problems would make him quick to see religious questionings, and of the particular kind that troubled himself, at the bottom of any man's difficulties. But nothing outside the man himself, not even the Tractarian controversy, is enough to account for such a state of mind as Clough's. It is something in the working of the mind that is at fault in such cases. Clough's mind was perplexed, not because the problems it was confronted with were heavy, but because they were light, not because it had too much on it, but because it had too little on it. At Rugby Clough had many things to do, and did them all well, and looked about for more things to do. At Oxford, lacking responsibility, and prevented by the system of things from acquiring it, he lacked interest in doing things, lacked therefore things to do, and the few things that he did, did rather badly. He took to thinking, instead ; and from the least sceptical of schoolboys changed to the most speculative of college men.

But not only was there too little leading for Clough to do at Oxford : there was also too little studying to do. His own ripest comment on his situation in this respect is to be found in a review which he wrote of the Oxford University Commissioners' Report of 1852. In an extract from this review which is printed in the *Prose Remains*, there occurs an approving account of the course of study at Rugby, followed by the exclamation that no words could express the amount of the change from Rugby to Oxford. " Had I not read," he asks, " pretty nearly all the books ? Was I to go on, keeping up my Latin prose writers, for three years more ? Logic and Ethics had some little novelty ; there was a little extra scholarship to be obtained in some of the college lectures. But that was the utmost.— I had been pretty well sated of distinctions and competitions at school ; I would gladly have dispensed with anything more of success in this kind, always excepting the £200 of the Fellowship. What I wanted was to sit down to happy, unimpeded prosecution of some new subject or subjects.—An infinite lassitude and impatience, which I saw reflected in the faces of others, quickly began to infect me. *Quousque* Latin prose ? " An impossible desire of Ward's—that Clough " should have given himself up thoroughly to his classical and mathematical studies."

Not much evidence remains of the plunge into theological controversies to which Ward ascribes Clough's comparative neglect of his studies. Clough himself said, much later, that for two years he had been " like a straw drawn up by the draught from a chimney." These two years would appear to have been the first of his university residence. The letters

from these years are not numerous, but in those few
there is no sign of a pronounced addiction to New-
manistic ideas. In May 1838 he writes to his
Cambridge friend Gell: " It is no harm, but rather
good, to give oneself up a little to learning Oxford
people, and admiring their good points, which lie,
I suppose, principally in all they hold in opposition
to the Evangelical portion of society—the benefit
and beauty and necessity of forms—the ugliness of
feelings put on unnaturally soon, and consequently
kept up by artificial means, ever strained and never
sober." He runs on through the letter, condemning
one or two, but moderately commending more, of
the Tractarian positions, and concludes: " If I had
said a quarter of this to——, he would have set me
down at once for a thorough-going convert ad New-
manismum. But you will not be so rash ; and you
remember that you asked me to write about it."
A year later he writes to the same friend: " I found
that at Rugby I had been quite set down among
theological gossips as a Newmanist, but the impression was pretty well removed by the time I came
away." The earlier of these two letters opens with
the words: " One thing, I suppose, is clear—that
one must leave the discussion of Τὰ Νεανδρώπικα"
—his name for Newmanism—" all snug and quiet
for after one's degree." These are obviously not
expressions of a soul " drawn up like a straw by the
draught of a chimney." Either Clough remained
genuinely calm through the storm of Newmanism,

or he was very successful in dissimulating his excitement to his correspondents.

But if neither to tracts nor to books for schools, to what, then, was Clough devoting his first attention in his undergraduate years ? Not, apparently, to riotous living, nor to reading out of course, nor to complete indolence ; rather to developing that firmness and consistency of character which was the most remarkable thing about him in his later life. He fell down in his examinations, not because he had spent too little time in studying, but because he had done his studying with an eye to self-discipline rather than to the examinations. " The object of honours," he writes to his sister, after taking his second, " is to make men read and not to make them distinguished ; and if I have read, it is all the same whether I am distinguished or not, and, so far as I am concerned, perhaps better."

The same idea must have occurred to many men similarly situated, as an easy bit of self-consolation. But there is every reason to believe that it had a much more genuine validity for Clough. In the next letter which he wrote his sister, he apologized, it is true, for expressing it : " I hope you will not blab my bravado any further." But the bravado is really in the apology, and not in the utterance apologized for. Never after his schooldays was it necessary for Clough to *pretend* indifference to the outward signs of success ; his task was rather to pretend, to himself still more than to others, that he *did* care anything at all about them. The difference between apparent good and real good in men so occupied and weighed upon his mind, and caused him to commit himself so definitely to the one rather than to the other, that, in himself at any rate, he became quite unduly suspicious of the appearance of excellence.

He writes to some one that he regards the loss, or diminution, of his reputation for scholarship as a good thing. It might, he felt, have resulted in his maintaining a false opinion of himself. Clough was as far as any one from having an " itch for martyrdom " in the usual sentimental sense ; but he had a great deal of an intellectual and moral something of the sort. He was too much inclined to regard it as a guarantee of the rightness of a course of conduct that it should lead away from, rather than toward, the attainment of any concrete good. Such a thing it was to have made oneself the quintessential Rugbeian.

His manner of living at Balliol was decidedly ascetic. He lived in small rooms, first in the garret and then on the ground floor of his quadrangle ; and he went through at least one entire winter without any fire. He was alone much of the time, partly because his poverty led him to avoid incurring social obligations, but still more for the sake of reflection and of resolute carrying out of self-imposed programmes of work. In the last of his undergraduate years he lived in lodgings in a small cottage just off

the Oxford street which is named Holywell. The
Cherwell stream is near by, and in it, Principal
Shairp records, Clough went bathing every morning
during the winter. It was obvious to his friends
and to his family that a great mental struggle was
going on in him. But he sought no relief from bur-
dening any one else with his worries. Even the loss
he is said to have suffered of great quantities of brown
hair failed to deter him from keeping on, with considerable outward serenity, in the Spartan hardness
of his chosen way of life. " His one idea," says
Ward, " seemed always to be that he should to-day
do to-day's duty, and for the rest leave himself in
God's hands." For a university student to be faithful to such an idea as this is not the result of spontaneous impulse or of chance. Asceticism is the
road to such an attitude to life. It was the road
Clough took ; and he kept the road.

What Clough chiefly strove for at Oxford, then,
was not a First, but self-control. And since the
men who knew him well, and he himself, are sufficiently agreed that he won the self-control, his
undergraduate career stands as a success in spite
of his loss of the First. It was a success of a kind
of which Clough was to win two or three more in the
rest of his life. These successes went unrewarded
except by themselves and by the affectionate and
respectful appreciation of a circle of good friends, a
number of them distinguished. They stand now as
the unmistakable marks of a character of the very

highest and strongest type. The first of them, of
course, was the greatest. What it meant was that
Clough had already as an undergraduate freed
himself from all other criteria of conduct than his
own sense of duty. Newman has celebrated the
phrase that represented to him the intuition on which
he came to base all truth and conduct : " Securus
judicat orbis terrarum." Clough was not imagina-
tive like Newman. The strong force in him was his
individual conscience. It was in his conscience
therefore that he found his test of truth. A motto
for him in form parallel to Newman's would require
for *orbis terrarum* some such words as *conscientia
individua fortis*.

To find the relief that any normal person must
desire from the spectacle of the tense life of the
ascetic, it is necessary to regard Clough when he is
away from Oxford, spending his holidays in Liverpool. He seems never to have been burdened with
the usual disposition of the seeker after perfection to be hard on the frailties of those around
him, or of the artist to concede to some one else the
privilege of standing as a firm reliance in time of
great troubles or small. The issues that he attended
to in his speculation and his poetry were vast ;
but he could always enter naturally and sympathetic-
ally into the everyday lives of his people, and be
really interested in all that was happening to them.

The verse Clough wrote in his undergraduate
days runs to hardly more than ten pages in his

published works, and of that total something near
half was probably composed in the months immediately following his taking of a degree. In these
early Oxford poems as in those done at Rugby
it is obvious that Clough's poet is Wordsworth.
One or two of them, " In a Lecture Room " and the
sonnet, " The Shady Lane," are pure Wordsworth.
A good deal of Wordsworth was always to remain
with Clough—a good deal of his simplicity of feelings
and words. In the early poems there is much of
the elder poet's feeling for nature—in his later work
this feeling gives way to something much closer
to the ordinary man's pleasure in outdoor life. The
morality of these verses sounds much like Wordsworth, but more still, in most cases, like Dr. Arnold.
It is less emotional and æsthetic, that is, and more
intellectual and voluntary. Something of romantic *weltschmerz* comes out in the pieces called " Re-
vival " and " A Song of Autumn." There is nothing
from first to last that the Oxford Movement can
possibly be considered to have inspired. There is
no single echo of the sweetness and the subtlety
of *The Christian Year* and *Lyra Apostolica.*

Nor is there anything in the substance of these
poems that can certainly be said to have proceeded
from the conflict into which Keble and Newman
had plunged the University. Possibly the emotions
which that conflict temporarily excited in the breast
of Clough were too intense to be represented in verse ;
and if later he made any attempt to " recollect

D

them in tranquillity," in accordance with the formula of his master, he found, even very shortly after his recovery of calm, that they no longer meant anything for him. For it was only during a very short period that Clough's problem was Newman or anti-Newman—Newman or Arnold. He came early to see that Newman and Arnold were both on the same side in the conflict that was really fundamental, that was *his* conflict—the conflict between common sense and open-mindedness on the one hand and, on the other, adherence to any set of principles that had been set up and were kept up by deliberate action of the will. What it comes to to say that " Oxford is the home of lost causes," is that Oxford is the home, for England, of this second kind of thinking—thinking that is tested by reference not to things as they are actually going on in the real world, but to things as they go on in an ideal world. Newman and Arnold were both, in this respect, typical Oxford thinkers. Clough's emotions and his imagination went out to these men, to Oxford, and to Oxford ways ; but his extraordinarily honest and persistent mind pulled him steadily in the opposite direction.

It is interesting to see what implications each of the two ways of thinking between which he vacillated had for Clough in respect to his own conduct. He very definitely associated action with the acceptance of one or the other of the two sets of principles, Newman's or Arnold's. Open-minded-

ness, on the other hand, meant to him a kind of
quietism, a patient waiting for a revelation, which—
—quite unempirically, indeed—he felt was absolutely
certain to come. Conduct was a matter for him almost wholly of expressing opinions, of entering
actively into the controversies of Oxford, and of
enlightening, mainly through poetry, we may suppose, the world outside the walls. Before he could
get to work at these tasks he must have settled
opinions. He could have these at the expense of
submitting his judgment to his own will, with
Arnold, or to his will submitted in turn to an
organized expression of will outside himself, with
Newman. But to place will above judgment was
a step he was temperamentally incapable of taking.
He simply was one of those who in the last resort
trust in the power of reason, and can believe that
reason is divine more easily than they can believe
will is divine. Will to Clough was his human self;
to accept and reject opinions by an act of will was
to commit the deadly sin of Pride.

It is this pride that he is crying out against, striving
to throw off, in the poem called " The Higher
Courage " :

> " Come back again, my olden heart !
>   Alas, I called not then for thee ;
> I called for Courage, and apart
>   From Pride if Courage could not be,
>   Then welcome, Pride ! "

The mood of pride and will is the mood, appar-

ently, of Clough's temporary inclination to go with
the Newmanists. He longs for the days of his
devotion to Arnold as a time of wise passivity and
acceptance, because that earlier devotion was not
a willed matter, but spontaneous. Dogmatism is
strong ; but he hates, and refuses, to will himself
into any form of it. He seems really hopeful of
recovering his early unawareness that the time
comes in this world, at any rate for all such thinkers
as he, when it is absolutely necessary to inject the
will, deliberately, into the making of decisions.
The higher courage is the courage to remain rudder-
less among shifting currents, to appear to other
men to be indecisive and lacking in convictions.

> " Come back again, old heart ! Ah me !
> Methinks in those thy coward fears
> There might, perchance, a courage be,
> That fails in these the manlier years ;
> Courage to let the courage sink,
> Itself a coward base to think,
> Rather than not for heavenly light
> Wait on to show the truly right."

The side of Clough which, even in this time of
extremest doubt and hesitation, thirsted for action,
finds expression in the poem with the Greek title,
" χρυσέα κλῂς ἐπὶ γλώσσᾳ "—" A Golden Key on
the Tongue." Here is voiced, for the first time
specifically, a longing for the turmoil of the real
outside world, for human relations, and work, and
excitement. Not on Poesy, nor revery, nor on
" some vain mate " is life to be wasted :

> " Heaven grant the manlier heart, that timely, ere
>   Youth fly, with life's real tempest would be coping;
>   The fruit of dreamy hoping
>   Is, waking, blank despair."

A sufficiently blank state of despair is revealed in the nine short pieces, mainly sonnets, grouped together under the head of " Blank Misgivings of a Creature moving about in Worlds not realized." Remorse is the sustained note in these, in spite of the outward appearance of blamelessness in Clough's early life. Listlessness and inactivity are abundantly regretted, but the principal source of pain is the conviction of having lived a lie :

> " How often sit I, poring o'er
>   My strange distorted youth,
>   Seeking in vain, in all my store,
>   One feeling based on truth."

A sickening lack of correspondence is discovered between the circumstances of the outer and those of the inner life. The acts and speeches of daily life fail utterly to reach

> " The buried world below."

Sometimes the expression of discontent takes obviously imitated forms, with no truth at all in them for Clough himself, as when he is so Byronic as to say :

> " I pace about the pathways of the world,
>   Plucking light hopes and joys from every stem."

Such a notion of himself, even when copied from another, is encouraging as one of the few signs of

an imagination in the early Clough. Very moral,
and not at all æsthetic, is the strong religious feeling
of this series of verses. God is the God of Arnold,
and trust in him is complete. The upshot of these
exercises in self-searching is the necessity of contentment and self-esteem in the performance of daily
tasks.

" Τὸ καλόν " is a better known expression of the
same conclusion, in somewhat more philosophical
form. " The Summum Pulchrum," Clough assures
us, not at all beautifully, " rests in heaven above,"
and will some day become visible to those who work
hard. More interesting is " The Music of the World
and of the Soul." It is interesting because it makes
clear a curious inversion, or seeming inversion, which
the Clough of these years came quite naturally to
make. There are two musics, he says:

> " One loud and bold and coarse,
> And overpowering still perforce
> All tone and tune beside ;
> Yet in despite its pride
> Only of fumes of foolish fancy bred,
> And sounding solely in the sounding head :
> The other, soft and low,
> Stealing whence we not know."

The first, of course, the music of the world, the second
of the soul. But to Clough, the world is really
Oxford, sometimes taken to be the principal earthly
manifestation of soul ; and by what he calls the soul
he really means the world. Oxford was the actual,
soiled, everyday thing ; human life outside the walls,

the divine mystery—Oxford, the low thing ; ordinary human existence, the high. To remain in the University was to be cowardly, to go out was to be brave. The problem was complicated by considerations of immediate duty, as problems always are ; but it remained at the back of all Clough's thinking, until he finally solved it, in the only possible way, by leaving Oxford.

It might have been better for Clough if he had gone out from Oxford immediately upon securing his degree. But he was very plainly marked for a trial at least of the academic life. He had no special preparation, and no interest in preparing himself, for any other profession than teaching. He was too uncertain of his beliefs to go into the Church. His family was too poor to provide him with a good business opening. He was all unready for the world, from ignorance of it, from over-development of his faculty of moral criticism, and from an utter lack of esteem for the tricks, as he regarded them, of conduct and expression which were the only means of convincing the world of the existence in himself of the unusual powers he was so confident he possessed.

A strong motive of a positive sort for remaining was the hope of redeeming the reputation he had lost by missing his First. He was doomed to be a don ; and if that fate, while it held for him, intensified his theological worries and gave him an unhappy feeling of repression, it gave him on the other hand plenty of time for thinking through the problems which it would have been necessary in any case for him to think through before he could attain anything like contentment.

The summer after his examination Clough spent with his family in Liverpool, occupying himself with some private pupils sent him by Dr. Arnold. In the fall he returned to Oxford, where he lived, as he had been living, on his scholarship and exhibition. He tried for a Balliol fellowship and lost. The disappointment was possibly greater than the disappointment of the spring. The force of such blows to youthful self-esteem is cumulative ; and while the practical value of a First was uncertain, to miss a fellowship was to miss an assurance of a steady income. But if Clough lost spirit to any extent he recovered sufficiently to win in a competition for a fellowship in Oriel the next spring. A place on the Oriel foundation must have been little, if any, less agreeable to him than a place in his own college. Besides having a name in scholarship second only to that of Balliol, Oriel was the college of Dr. Arnold, as well as of Newman, and there came to it as fellow some years later the younger Arnold. Principal Shairp records that Newman assisted in the examination of Clough, and that this was the last examination in which he took a part. To Clough the success was exceedingly gratifying. It removed the need for worry about his immediate future ; but it was still more valuable as a vindication.

CHAPTER IV

AS FELLOW OF ORIEL

THE external life that Clough led at Oxford was as placid and as regular as his inner life was intense and exceptional. His love of outdoor living was even beyond that of the usual Oxford man, but it took no unusual forms. He went on long walks and rowed and swam, and whenever he could, spent a week or a month or a season in the hills of Wales or Scotland. These enterprises provided him with a host of minor experiences—glimpses of the beauty of nature, unobstructed revelations of the soul processes of his companions, moments of rare acquiescence in the scheme of things and in himself. He lacked the impulse to isolate an occasional incident of one of these varieties, and to transmute it into a poem. His short pieces are abstract. His longer poems, on the other hand, are quite full of his minor experiences, used apparently with very little reshaping. But there was nothing in his own experience dramatic enough, or persistent enough, to provide a connective principle adequate to a work of art. Hence in devising a plot he always took his main thread from imagined experience which under the circumstances provided by actual minor incidents he might have met with, but had not met with. So in *The Bothie* he interests himself mainly in philanderings and more legitimate affairs with Scottish maidens, although the unanimous indication of all that he and others wrote about his Highland sojourns is that he invariably did his admiring of the lassies from a safe distance.

All his life Clough had admiring friends, in whose eyes he cut a very impressive figure. The praises of him that these friends published after his death were so warm as to produce in the general mind—always incredulous on such points—rather more doubt than certainty of his excellences. For no stage of his life are these praises warmer than for the time when he was making the transition from scholar to fellow. He was not nearly so widely known as he had been at Rugby. His insistence on holding aloof from the Tractarian struggle, on doing his thinking for himself, lost him his opportunity for becoming a University celebrity. But in his own college he was the object of profound respect, most of it, even from those who were then and afterward his best friends, of a distant kind. He was looked upon as one marked for greatness, and was therefore, of course, something of a joke with the irreverent, who yet, for all their flippancy, appear to have shared in the general admiration of him.

What he had come to be in physical appearance is specifically described by his friend the poet Allingham : " Clough was five feet ten in height, well made, inclining to burliness ; he had a handsome frank

face, dark-eyed, full-chinned and ruddy-complex-
ioned, the nose being straight and rather short ;
his head, which was early bald, ran deep from front
to back, and showed a graceful domed outline."
Other descriptions find his chin irresolute and
his mouth sweet rather than firm. A poetical portrait of him is provided by Principal Shairp, in the
poem "Balliol Scholars" which he wrote in 1875 :

" Foremost one stood, with forehead high and broad,—
    Sculptor ne'er moulded grander dome of thought,—
Beneath it, eyes dark-lustred rolled and glowed,
    Deep wells of feeling where the full soul wrought ;
Yet lithe of limb, and strong as shepherd boy,
He roamed the wastes and drank the mountain joy,
    To cool a heart too cruelly distraught."

In a prose contribution to the *Memoir*, Shairp mentions massiveness of figure as one of the strongest
impressions given by Clough. His health and vigour
through these Oxford years were exceptional. A
contributing cause for the slenderness of his poetic
product may be detected in the nature and extent
of his physical power, which was of a sort to make
for a measure of stolidity. He was keen and taut,
but his stimuli came from within. He was not
extraordinarily alive to impressions, as he should
have been satisfied that he was before proposing
to himself a poetic career. And, indeed, poetry appears to have occupied in his mind a place definitely
secondary to that held by his academic occupations.

Clough loved to teach; there can be no doubt of
that. The didactic impulse had been strong in him

from the age of fourteen or so. But it impelled in these maturer years a very different sort of teaching. To the younger boys at Rugby Clough had laboured to impart a quite positive and definite religious and moral dogma. At Oxford his point of view was critical, and more and more sceptical ; his method, however, only very cautiously socratic. Not even with his friends, much less with his pupils, does he seem to have pressed his attack on an opinion which seemed to him false much farther than by a mild question or two to instil an initial doubt of it. Yet such was the impression he gave of sound judgment and of a reserved store of argument that even so gentle an assault on error seems in many cases to have been singularly effective. " Several survivors," says Mr. Bagehot, " may think they owe much to Mr. Clough's quiet question, ' Ah, then you think—— ? ' "

The work done in the school of *Litterae Humaniores* at Oxford was, and is, extraordinarily remote from the facts and principles of actual life. If this had not been true, Clough would probably have enjoyed still less peace of mind during his work at Oriel. His hypertrophied conscience felt keenly the fact that he was employed by an institution closely connected with the Church. If his duties had involved much discussion of living opinions in religion and politics, that conscience would never have permitted him to undermine by questioning opinions which he was bound not to oppose directly. As it was his tutorial hours concerned themselves with Thucydides, and the Athenian Tragedy, and Latin Prose Composition. Even so the time came soon enough when Clough was to feel his formal adherence to the religion of his college as an unendurable restraint on his mental activity.

There were other forces than love of the tutor's task which operated to hold Clough at Oxford. In the first place, inertia, a very strong argument indeed with a man who made decisions with such great difficulty. Then he loved Oxford. Unlike most poets, he did his living in the world actually about him, and not in any world of dreams. The objects of his emotions, so far as they were persons and places at all, were *real* persons and places. Oxford did not have to suffer by comparison with any city of the sun or of the moon. Third, he saw himself as a player, though an humble one, of the intellectual game ; and the desire was natural to remain on the field where, for England, that game was being played most zealously.

But all of these bonds might not have held Clough at Oxford year after year had not the need of money which first led him to work for a fellowship been aggravated, not lessened, by the course of events. His father failed in business in 1841, and lost most of his money. It became necessary for Mrs. Clough and her daughter to do most of their own household work. The responsibility fell upon Arthur Clough of keeping up some part of the expenses, as well as the courage and happiness of his people. The family had experience of death in these years as well as of poverty. In 1842 the youngest son, George, went out to Charleston on his father's business, and after only a few months there was taken sick of the fever and died. The father had sailed for America a short time after the son, and with no knowledge of his illness. He was met at Boston with the news of his loss, which affected him so heavily as to hasten his own end. The boy was only twenty-two, and he was particularly bright and engaging. He had suffered his last illness far from home. Furthermore, he had been counted on to straighten out the increasing business difficulties of his father. The elder Mr. Clough returned to England in the summer of 1843, grief stricken and ill ; and after months of helplessness died in November of the next year.

Through this unhappy period Clough spent much of his time at home. The house at Liverpool remained a home to him in the fullest sense. Loving reality always, he found more of it in domestic life than in academic. He did not avert his attention from poverty and grief and death ; nor did he allow them to unsettle his nerves, or bring about any sudden changes in his way of looking at life. Yet it is quite evident that the sorrows and anxieties of this time affected him profoundly. His mind seized on the problems of mortality and evil that they presented, not to cast them aside in pain, not to conceal them under some elaborate metaphysical ornamentation, not to dispose of them by any hasty imperative, but to turn them over and over, to regard them steadily and from every possible angle, and in the end to profess only to have become used to them, not to have become master of them.

Anne Jemima Clough kept a journal through these years, which is printed, in part, in a Memoir of her by her niece. In this journal Miss Clough speaks often of her brother, and always very lovingly and admiringly. Nothing delights her so much as his homecomings, nothing strengthens her so much as his counsels. " He is the comfort and joy of my life," she writes ; " it is for him and from him that I am incited to seek after all that is lovely and of good report. Preach no sermons, give no precepts, but set before me a holy, beautiful example, and my heart will burn within me, and I shall surely long and strive to follow it." The journal reveals Miss Clough as no less resolute than her brother in searching for the right way of life. She decided early that the way for her would not be the usual way for women. There were not then many good examples for a woman to follow in seeking to do a work of her own in the world, not many women to go to for advice. And so Miss Clough set her brother to thinking about the subject of woman's work. They talked about it a great deal. They were together not only in Clough's holidays at home, but during visits his sister made him at Oxford and on journeys in which she accompanied him. He took her through the Lake country one summer, and in 1846 to Europe. They went up the Rhine to Switzerland, and spent some time among the Italian lakes.

The deaths of a father and of a brother were preceded by another great loss, felt perhaps no less poignantly. Dr. Arnold died quite suddenly in 1842, at the early age of forty-seven. "He was for a long time more than a father to me," said Clough ; and left Oxford on hearing the news, and went home, and thence to the Welsh hills for a period of solitary wandering. This was a death to have the strongest effect on his thinking ; for the life it ended in its prime must still have appeared to him the most unquestionably useful life in all England. It had this particular effect on his thinking, that it left him alone in the world as no other death could have done. Love of Dr. Arnold was a powerful chain holding him to some sort of conformity with the Church, and to a feeling of obligation to bring honour to Rugby in some one of the conventional ways. The breaking of the chain not so much set Clough free to go his own way, as enforced on him the necessity of finding a way that could be his own.

"I am, right or wrong," writes Clough in one of the letters of this time, "as a matter of fact, exceedingly averse to act on anything but what I have got from myself." The record of his life at Oxford is a record of progressive isolation of spirit. It is the sad experience of most men that solitary confinement is an established principle in the prison whose shades close so rapidly on the growing boy. But Clough deliberately sought to isolate himself. From being a passionate disciple he became a passionate individualist. This individualism, however, was in itself a discipleship. Clough had heard the great voice of Carlyle. There inhered in the message of that voice an effective veto on any outward profession of discipleship on the part of one who really heard it and accepted it. For no one really hears and accepts the recommendation to the many, to be disciples : what every one attends to is the lesson to the few—to be heroic, and to think for oneself. If Jones is persuaded by Smith to do his thinking for himself, it is in the nature of the case that for him to call Smith Master would be a poor way of expressing his gratitude. Hence we do not find Clough commending Carlyle's books in his letters, nor talking about Old Clothes and Great Silent Men. Yet the most satisfactory understanding of Clough's singular inaction and watchfulness in these years is to be gained by seeing that he was proposing to be himself a Great Silent Man, and that while he appeared to be doing nothing, he was in fact sedulously ridding his spirit of its Old Clothes, and preparing himself, alas, in vain, for the pealing through all the recesses of his being of his own " Everlasting Yea."

R. H. Hutton, who knew Clough, insists, in a magazine article which he wrote about him, and later

E

reprinted, on the great importance of this Carlylean influence. He says it was Carlyle's injunction to men to clear their lives of misleading pretensions that led Clough to leave Oxford ; and to show that Clough ultimately became dissatisfied with the Silent Man theory of life, he quotes him as saying : " Carlyle led us out into the wilderness and left us there." This appears to have been a favourite remark with Clough : he made it also to Emerson, when he was seeing him off for America at the Liverpool docks in 1848. And Emerson told Edward Everett Hale that many other young Englishmen had said the same thing to him.

Up to the time when he found himself thus left in the wilderness, Clough followed very faithfully. He was one of a number that is fortunately very small, in carrying his devotion to the point of writing Carlylese. He does this sometimes in his letters, but very notably in a pamphlet which he published in 1847 on the subject of Retrenchment (of private expenses) at Oxford : " Who wants ices with the wind N.N.E. ; who likes Nuneham or Godstowe in the rain ? When all the watering-pots of heaven are playing upon High Street, there will hardly be a quorum for examining one's toilet. With the roses and the May will come out, I greatly fear, the champagne and the claret.—For my own part, if the corn could only ripen in it, I could wish for rain and cold to the end of the chapter." In a following paragraph he expresses a fear that in this passage rhetoric has led him astray " into the limbo of the factitious." And indeed it has led him astray throughout the article. He cannot rise to the immense contempt which Carlyle would have felt for undergraduate claret and waistcoats and Ireland starving. He is left hanging, only half-way up from the much gentler sarcasm that was his own style of humour.

Humour, however, whether in his own style or another's—and in so far as he ever possessed any of it—was to develop in Clough later. Certainly it played very little part in the all-too-serious life which he led at Oxford. And his prose style was not then, nor did it ever become, a matter of significance, aside from its betrayal of the influence under which he was doing his thinking. His artistic interest was in verse, and in verse of the soberest, least humorous kind. There is not much of this verse—only some score of short pieces. Clough gathered them up at the end of his stay at Oxford, and printed them, together with some of his earlier poems, in a volume called *Ambarvalia* which he got out in 1849 in connection with his old Rugby friend, the Reverend Thomas Burbidge. These Oxford poems of Clough's —except indeed for one piece written in honour of a silver wedding—have nothing whatever to do with the outside world. They are purely introspective. There are only two subjects : half of them are about Duty, and the other half about God.

It is some of the ethical poems that are most read

to-day ; but for a study of Clough himself the
religious poems are the more interesting.   There are
three of these last that are particularly fine.   All
three voice the same notion of God ; all ring with
the same intensity of feeling, the same immense
sincerity.   The view of God is that of a spirit dwelling
in the human spirit.   The feeling is that passionate
straining after nobler things which was inculcated
in Clough by his mother and then strengthened by the
successive influences of Arnold and Newman and
Carlyle.   In the sincerity there is perhaps to be
seen much that was peculiar to Clough's individual
temperament : this, for instance, that he thought
too much about the final outcome of his search for
truth—worried about it ; and this worry interfered
with the search, as lessening the amount and the
coolness of the attention he had left to bestow on
the particular successive steps of it. Yet it is the
need for cool deliberation that he is always talking
about.

In the first of these poems, " The New Sinai "
(1845), Clough is crying out his scorn of man's weak
desire to see his god in first this and then that person
or thing in the phenomenal world.   Once, on Sinai,
God had rebuked this frailty, saying, " I am One."
But the lesson went unheeded :

> " And baby-thoughts again, again,
> Have dogged the growing man."

Man's present need is resolutely to reject all that

remain of the long line of man-created images of God
—and create a new and better image, would be
Carlyle's message, but Clough insists on a termination
of the image-building process. Once more God will
speak authoritatively to man, but out of man's
own spirit, if man will but prepare that spirit.
Meanwhile,

> "And wait it out, O Man!"

is Clough's counsel. There is a singular resemblance
at this point between the position of the over-intel-
lectual Oxford tutor and that of the untaught Primitive Methodist or Seventh Day Adventist. The one
was as sure in his mind as the other is in his heart
of a Second Coming. As violent, almost, as the
emotional fanaticism which he had been taught to
hate, was Clough's old Rugbeian faith in the efficacy
of clear and clean religious thinking. One thing,
at any rate, that thinking had now established.
Clough's old debate with himself over the possibility
of accepting by an act of the will such a God as
Newman's was finally settled. Already in 1843
Clough had had great difficulty in bringing himself
to sign the Articles. His willingness to associate
himself with any form of dogma became from that
time steadily less and less.

The second of these poems, " Qui Laborat, Orat,"
has the distinction, first of all, of showing the very
best that Clough could do in the way of expression
—and that best, in a rather unambitious way, very
good indeed. It is one of the great Victorian poems.

It succeeds in stating quite plainly, and with no single unnecessary word, a sequence of profound, yet simple, ideas ; and at the same time in attaining a severe but beautiful melody to convey the deep emotional quality which inheres in those ideas. It was several times rewritten, but dashed off in the first instance, as Thomas Arnold tells, during the hours of a sleepless night which Clough passed at Arnold's London lodgings after a long evening's talk with him on the subject of prayer.

It seems quite unlikely that Carlyle's great exhortation in *Past and Present* to labour as the best sort of prayer can have been out of Clough's mind when he wrote his verses. *Past and Present* had just been printed : of course Clough had been reading it. It is not at all true, however, that he simply makes poetry of Carlyle's prose. His statement, indeed, is so much the clearer, and cooler, and more logical of the two that it might at least as well be said that he makes prose of Carlyle's poetry. But with each man it is true that both idea and form are poetic, though the difference in idea is only less great than the difference in form. Clough's argument for worship through work is quite another thing from Carlyle's argument. To work is to pray with Carlyle, because it is the bravest, hardest, spiritually wholesomest thing a man may do ; but with Clough, because it is that thing a man may do which is least likely to be bold, to be profane, or to be—horror of horrors, always—factitious ;

> " With eye down-dropt, if then this earthly mind
>   Speechless remain, or speechless e'en depart ;
> Nor seek to see—for what of earthly kind
>   Can see Thee as Thou art ?
>
> If well assured 'tis but profanely bold
>   In thought's abstractest forms to seem to see ;
> It dare not dare the dread communion hold
>   In ways unworthy Thee.
>
> O not unowned Thou shalt unnamed forgive,
>   In worldly walks the prayerless heart prepare ;
> And if in work its life it seem to live,
>   Shalt make that work be prayer."

Not inferior are the verses to which Clough gave
the name " ὕμνος ἄμνος." He himself, never inclined
to value his own works very highly nor very long,
seems to have been well pleased with this work. At
any rate he writes of it, from America, at least four
or five years later, to the lady who was to become
his wife : "It wants a good deal of mending as it
stands, but it is on the whole in sense very satisfactory
to me still." It received the mending, and stands
as an excellent example of the perfect straightfor-
wardness and sincerity of Clough's style :

> " O Thou, in that mysterious shrine
>   Enthroned, as I must say, divine !
> I will not frame one thought of what
>   Thou mayest either be or not.
> I will not prate of ' thus ' and ' so,'
>   And be profane with ' yes ' and ' no,'
> Enough that in our soul and heart
>   Thou, whatsoe'er Thou mayest be, art."

In connection with his frequent exhortations to
action it strikes a reader continually that Clough did

not practise what he preached ; but the resolution about his thinking which he here makes he seems to have kept pretty well. Having framed, up to this time in his life, an altogether exceptional number of thoughts about the nature of God, and having reached, at any rate, a considerable number of negative conclusions, he brought this research at last almost, if not quite, to an end. It only remained for him to doubt whether there is any god at all of any sort. This doubt Clough was to experience in full force ; for several years his mind was full of it. A *modus vivendi* resulted, in time, which consisted in refusing to admit any validity to any man's way of conceiving God, refusing to formulate any new way of conceiving God, and yet living always and talking sometimes in the manner of a devout believer in God.

The only thing peculiar to himself about this position of Clough's was the extreme arduousness of the path by which he arrived at it. His God had been Arnold's God, really, all the time—the God of most of the thoughtful members of the great Latitudinarian section of the Church, with their poverty of dogma and their fine wealth of Christian feeling. He was the God of the Unitarians, and of many of the Independents ; Clough recognized his own congeniality with the best Nonconformist thinking, and mentions in one or two of his letters more or less serious notions that possessed him at times of becoming an Independent parson. But whereas most of those who held this substantially identical theology had adopted it with their eyes resolutely averted from the central mystery to problems of conduct and to opportunities for carefully controlled emotion, Clough had faced and travelled straight forward. Brave and patient and pure of heart, he had fought his way on. He had gone as far toward finding God as a citizen of his age, travelling by the intellect, could go. And now that he had come to the end, there was a certain flatness, hardly less disconcerting for the fact that he had partly anticipated it, about the goal which he had reached. He felt as Admiral Peary may well have felt in coming upon a North Pole which was after all only a point to be approximately ascertained in a field of ice quite devoid of landmarks. Nothing remained for either explorer to do except to turn back to more habitable regions —back to a temperate zone, where the business of living was actually being carried on without much dependence on the nature of ultimate things, either terrestrial or spiritual.

Clough states this religious position of his very candidly in a letter to his sister written from Oxford in 1847. He gets into the subject through talk of reading Coleridge. "My own feeling," he writes, " does not go along with Coleridge in attributing any special virtue to the facts of Gospel history. . . . And I do not think that doubts respecting the facts related in the gospels need give us much trouble. . . . Trust in God's justice and love, and belief in His

commands as written in our conscience, stand un-
shaken, though Matthew, Mark, Luke, and John, or
even St. Paul, were to fall." Later in the letter,
in answer to his own question, " What is the meaning
of ' Atonement by a crucified Saviour ' ? " he says :
" That there may be a meaning in it, which shall
not only be consistent with God's justice, that is,
with the voice of our conscience, but shall be the
very perfection of that justice, the one true expression
of our relations to God, I don't deny ; but I do deny
that Mr. M'Neile, or Mr. Close, or Dr. Hook, or
Pusey, or Newman himself, quite know what to
make of it. The Evangelicals gabble at it, as the
Papists do their Ave Marys, and yet say they know ;
while Newman falls down and worships *because* he
does not know, and knows he does not know." And
of his own attitude : "If I am not born with the power
to discover " (Clough's belated disillusionment consisted in his acceptance of the fact that he lacked
this power), " I will do what I can with what knowledge I have—trust to God's justice, and neither
pretend to know, nor, without knowing, pretend to
embrace : nor yet oppose those who, by whatever
means, are increasing or trying to increase knowledge." A little harsh, perhaps, are the references
to Newman and the Evangelicals. Yet considering
the long predominance of his religious feeling, and
the intensity of his old hope of finding God, the
amount of bitterness of spirit in the Clough of these
years cannot but be regarded as admirably slight,

and admirably controlled. There is no defiance in his rejection of the accepted faiths, no setting up of a counter-dogma, no closed-mindedness. On the contrary, the succeeding period of his life shows a very rapid increase in him of tolerance, of openness of mind, of humanity.

An interesting ethical parallel to this widening down of his religious feeling is to be found in Clough's treatment in another letter of the same month of a problem of discipline which his sister had submitted to him. She had been grieved by the appearance of petty stealing among the children of her school. Clough argues the matter very gravely, urging especially that pilfering is natural to children. He goes on to tell, with a singular *naïveté* for a man of twenty-eight addressing another adult, that he has a friend who stole a book from a shop while he was a schoolboy and has never returned it, but has kept it openly on his shelves, letting his friends know how he came by it. " Well," comments the erstwhile moral Clough, " I don't think worse of him on the whole for this ; I respect him for his present frankness ; and though I think he ought to have gone afterwards and told the bookseller, and paid him, yet I don't think it's very much matter." To such a pass had the slack life of Oxford brought a sterling Rugby conscience ! It was yet not so far gone but that Clough shuddered somewhat at his own depravity. He has the grace to apologize for his advice, " which I dare say, or rather I am sure, mother, and I dare say you will not think quite high-principled."

This liberalization of Clough's ideas was not, so far as his writings show, either produced or attended by any strengthening of his sense of humour. Up to the last of his Oxford days he took himself and his problems with complete seriousness. Or if the sceptical second self which interested him so much later existed also in this earlier time, it did not at any rate find expression. Clough did not yet allow a place in his mind to the mocking spirit which broke out in Dipsychus. It was not mockery but earnest thinking which brought about his slow decline from the highest transcendentalism. Yet this is not to say that his Oxford experience was made up of nothing but high thinking. The life of a don was not without its amenities even in those days of bitter controversy. And in Clough's later years at the University religious excitement had so far died down as to permit of a general reawakening of interest in such things as politics, and social theories, and foreign affairs, and the arts—an awakening which Clough shared in a manner that was very important for his own life if not for the life of the community.

Clough's new interest in affairs found expression in his talk and his letters, of course, but also in the activities of a small but distinguished debating society called the Decade. This society appears to have been made up mainly of young Fellows of Oriel and Balliol. It was founded in 1840, with a membership limited to ten ; this limit was later disregarded, and yet through the entire ten years that the society lasted it had scarcely thirty members. Some of these members were Jowett, Tait, Church, John Duke Coleridge, Thomas and Matthew Arnold, Shairp, Conington, Chichester Fortescue, F. T. Palgrave, and Arthur Stanley. Of these men Church, Thomas Arnold, Shairp, Conington, Palgrave, Stanley, and Coleridge have written reminiscences of the work of the society ; and all agree that to Clough belonged a considerable prestige—indeed one of them says definitely the first place—in its debates. Stately, severe, deeply suggestive, deliberate, negligent of rhetorical flow, poetic in thought, possessed of a firm hold on reality, serene, original, and, of course, convincing—these are a few of the flattering characteristics ascribed to his manner of speaking. Accounts of particular discussions in which he shared indicate more than anything else the ability of a Hamlet to see quite too many sides of a question ever to reach any effective decision. He is sure of one thing—that Wordsworth is a greater poet than Tennyson ; and he supports philosophically the abstract and obvious proposition that the manufacturing interest, in view of its increase, should have increased political recognition. But on most issues he is set down as " neither for nor against," as " supporting in part," or as " supporting with qualifications." And when he combats *laissez-faire*, it is " with moderation."

What all of this comes to is that Clough was, as yet, indecisive. He was still doing his living on the inside of his own head. He was learning a good many facts and theories about the real life of the world, but he was using them only as pieces and pawns in his own little intellectual game, in his own private search for his own private truth. He was completely intellectualist—not in the least the pragmatist that he was later, in part at any rate, to become. He had no real appreciation as yet of the importance of movement. He talked about the prime necessity of action, but he really regarded action all the time as quite secondary to thought. Action was a sort of drug by which pain could be minimized during the long lapses between steps in the slow ascent of thinking. The test of the man, as well as the man himself, lay in the individual conscience. The " objective," to use the old words, could play only a deceptively real part in a world so completely " subjective."

Clough's friendships were not of a sort to provide correctives for the defects in this way of taking life. A few of the members of the Decade undoubtedly proved themselves later to be worthy of the name of men of action. But most of them were definitely men of reflection, and became tutors or heads of colleges, or clergymen. The men of this latter sort were likely to be Clough's intimates. The younger Thomas Arnold says that after he came up to Oxford " a little interior company " was formed

very well how far Clough stands on this side of Romanticism ; for friendship is a classical, a conventional, or anything else before a romantic subject, the value of friendship to a man being that it lessens, not enhances, his sense of the mystery, the foreignness, of the world about him. They call to mind, too, how particularly poignant the sense of the fleetingness of earthly associations, always present in the atmosphere of a university, must have been in the Oxford of these days, with the additional causes it had for the breaking of close ties in the quarrels brought on by the Movement. And they are further a reminder of the disappointment, peculiar to Clough, of seeing break into pieces and fly off into all directions, none perhaps so far aside as that which he himself took, the stout Rugby phalanx which his high youthful fancy had seen advancing, ever united and ever victorious, to the conquest of a world of sin. It is not therefore as a personal loss that he deplores parting, but as a most painful evidence of the difficulties of co-operation, the impossibility of keeping the good in the world all united for the contest with evil. There is something of the tone of Lycidas in the poems.

Less unromantic, it is agreeable to notice, are two early poems on Love. The romance in these, however, is not at all a matter of yearnings and despairs, of moonlight, nor of eyebrows. It is a matter of careful speculation—a single idea, in fact,

subtly developed : the idea that Love is the one
mysterious power which is to be obeyed even before
Duty and before Reason.

> " Men and maidens, see you mind it ;
> Show of love, where'er you find it,
> Look if duty lurk behind it !
> Duty-fancies, urging on
> Whither love had never gone ! "

It is a lyric not without charm, this awkwardly
named " Love, Not Duty," and it is interesting
as a consistent first utterance of a poet who wrote
much and thoughtfully about love and marriage,
from a point of view high and sane and considerably
in advance of his time. " Poet of Doubt " Clough
was named in the years, just after his death, when
Darwin's books were causing men to classify everything under the head of Doubt or the head of Belief.
Yet of his four main works, three, *The Bothie*,
Amours de Voyage, and *Mari Magno*, are concerned mainly with love ; and in the fourth,
Dipsychus, it appears to be principally because
the poem is incomplete that love plays a secondary
part. In these early lyrics he is a poet of love who
is not as yet making professed use of any experience
in the field that he may himself have accumulated.
Love exacts meditation from him as a beautiful
vision on the one hand, and as a serious responsibility on the other ; but there is nothing to indicate
a connection between this meditation and any parti-

cular case.   Everything Clough has to say about love is perfectly general :

> " A glory on the vision lay ;
>   A light of more than mortal day
>   About it played, upon it rested ;
>   It did not, faltering and weak,
>   Beg Reason on its side to speak :
>   Itself was Reason, or, if not,
>   Such substitute as is, I wot,
>   Of seraph-kind the loftier lot."

To all of which it might be urged that, whether begged or not, this is certainly Reason speaking on the side of Love.

But reason was speaking to Clough in these days much less frequently on the side of Love than on the side of Duty.   There was no conflict between the two : Love continued, apparently, to present no problems demanding solution, whereas Duty kept in the forefront all the time the problem, What to do with a life.   Clough seems to have been so greatly interested in the problem that he was reluctant to solve it and so have it out of his way. Yet he is continually expressing his confidence that Duty is the true guide, and that he has committed himself to following her guidance implicitly.   It is this which he is saying in a noteworthy poem of 1847, " The Questioning Spirit " ; and rather more explicitly and forcibly in a set of hexameters, done, perhaps, a little later :

" Go from the east to the west, as the sun and the stars direct
    thee ;
Go with the girdle of man, go and encompass the earth :
Not for the gain of the gold ; for the getting, the hoarding, the
    having,
But go for the joy of the deed ; but for the Duty to do.
Go with the spiritual life, the higher volition and action.
With the great girdle of God, go and encompass the earth."

Here seems to be a moderately specific and a
quite firmly established idea of what duty is. In
another poem, written, it appears, nearer the time
when the great decision of his life, to leave Oxford,
was being made, there begins the analysis of duty
which was to play so important a part in *Dipsychus*
and other later works. This poem, printed under
the name " Duty, " is the bitterest piece of irony
that Clough ever wrote. It is perhaps the only
thing he ever wrote that reveals unrestrained ill-
temper and a spirit of rebellion. It contemns the
current idea of duty :

" Duty—'tis to take on trust
   What things are good and right and just
   And whether indeed they be or not,
   Try not, test not, feel not, see not."

Back to his own higher notion of Duty the poet
rushes in the final verses :

" Duty !
  Yea, by duty's prime condition
    Pure nonentity of duty ! "

This is rough versifying, even for Clough ; but it
has a very satisfying freedom from the air of quiescence that mars much of Clough's work on themes in

the treatment of which quiescence is a highly undesirable quality.

It is disappointing to find in the poems of Clough's years of teaching at Oxford so little improvement over his undergraduate poems in respect to form— or perhaps it should be said rather, so little appearance of an increase of concern about form, since the considerable improvement that there is seems to proceed directly from a firmer grasp on ideas and a heightened emotional intensity, and not from any attention paid to expression itself. Imitation is a fault with most young poets, but Clough was not imitative enough. After his first boyish imitations of Wordsworth, he struck out for himself quite too negligently of teachers who might have given him much that he needed. This carelessness of the art of writing was a part of his sleepless suspicion of everything that was not the truth itself, truth about God or about Man. But it was a manifestation also of a lack in Clough's nature of verve and style, of a sense for grace and melody. It was a serious failing, and yet Clough, we may suppose, might have overcome it more successfully than he did, if he had put himself to school to the great poets of the preceding generation. But this there is every reason to believe it did not occur to him to do. It is as if he trusted all too far to Milton's dictum that he who would " write well hereafter in laudable things ought himself to be a true poem."

Refraining from imitation, if it stunted Clough's

craftsmanship on the one hand, helped to secure
to him, on the other, the genuine originality that
proceeds from almost perfect simplicity and unso-
phistication.   It has already been remarked of two
of his poems that they show a long advance from
the days of the romantic poets.   He never hunts
out subjects like theirs to write about, but always
writes out of the thoughts and feelings of his own
daily life, the daily life of a University man of
the second quarter of the century.   To such a conception of poetry the need for the poet to make his
life a true poem is a corollary.   There were other
reasons for Clough's determination to leave Oxford;
but one reason was persuasion that his cloistered
life was too narrow to be truly poetic.

CHAPTER V

THE BOTHIE OF TOBER-NA-VUOLICH

L EAVING Oxford was the most nearly dramatic thing Clough ever did. He gave up his tutorship in Oriel in April 1848, and his fellowship in October, with no promise and no very fair prospect of a position elsewhere. If Browning had added Clough to his dramatic portraits this is the episode in his life with which he would needs have been content. To Clough himself, reflecting over the act long and heavily, both before and after, it seemed enormously dramatic, however much he may have felt the necessity of making his departure modestly and quietly and of disparaging the boldness of it to himself as to others. At least one of his admirers is equally inclined to ascribe epochal significance to the move. " When Clough left Oxford," writes Charles Eliot Norton, " he had conquered his world. . . . Whatever might become of him, whatever he might become, his life was a success such as scarcely one man in a generation achieves." It was one of the chief disabilities of Clough for practical life that he shared this extravagant estimate of the almost wholly negative virtue of intellectual honesty.

What it came to in conduct was that he insisted on seeing himself as differing widely from groups of men with whom he was really in almost perfect agreement. The few points of difference he heeded and magnified because they were the proofs of his individuality. Above all things he thought it right, and he wanted, to become himself ; he was coming to see that the way to be himself was to get out of himself ; and the way to get out of himself was to get out of Oxford.

To remain seemed the practical thing no less certainly than to go was the ideal thing. A few shy inquiries about work in the outside world had been fruitless ; and to work in order to live was a necessity with Clough as well as a principle. He had not only to support himself, but must carry out an agreement he had entered into after his father's death. He had promised to pay a member of his family an annuity of £100 in return for the final reversion of a larger sum. He had the fixed, and for that reason if no other, valid opinion that he could not write rapidly, nor spontaneously ; and his conscience limited very severely the number of reviews to which he would permit himself to contribute. He speaks in one of his letters of the time of having determined to abandon verse for the writing of essays, presumably for economic reasons. But he seems to have felt in the main that his one chance of making a living lay in teaching. There were very few teaching positions outside of the University that were at all well paid or at all congenial, so few as to make Clough's decision to go forth into the world appear not merely bold but rash. It required immeasurably more courage than a similar decision would require to-day, in England, or especially in America.

An action of such consequence rested, of course, for a man like Clough, on a vast and complicated array of considerations. The thing that precipitated the problem was that remaining at Oxford meant not merely subscription to the Thirty-nine Articles but the taking of Holy Orders. A Charter provision concerning the original Fellowships of the Oriel foundation was that nine of them should be held by students of theology and three by students of common or canon law. Modern interpretation had converted this into a rule that Fellows of the first class should take Holy Orders, and those of the second, degrees in law or medicine. Clough's was a theological Fellowship, and he had held it for six years. The contingency of taking Orders he was presumably compelled to look upon as imminent. And he was not merely out of agreement with the particular principles that taking Orders would bind him to support ; he was continually confessing to his correspondents an utter weariness of the whole world of theological talk and ecclesiastical gossip.

With this difficulty was connected another, for which again responsibility lay chiefly with the

fourteenth century founders of the college. When
the reluctant Fellow had taken Orders it yet remained for him to choose between academic and
domestic life. It was practically impossible for
him to have both. In these years before successive
Parliamentary Commissions had as yet laid rough
hands on the University Statutes, it was only Heads
of Colleges and a very few other Senior Members
that were permitted to have wives. If Clough
wanted to marry—and *The Bothie* says nothing
if not that he did want to marry—his choice was
between breaking away from Oxford altogether on
the one hand, and on the other not only taking Orders
but accepting a benefice and actually conducting
church services.

It must also have counted for something with
Clough that he was almost as far out of sympathy
with the politics of the University as with its religion—which is to say that his divergence was
slight, by ordinary standards, but that he himself
considered it to be great and decisive. What
set him to thinking politically was the Irish famine
of 1847. An association had been formed to encourage economy among the undergraduates—more,
apparently, as a way of exhibiting sympathy with
the Irish than as an attempt at actually helping
to keep them alive. One of Clough's longer prose
works is a pamphlet discussing objections to this
movement. The work is typical of its author
in that it is impossible to classify it either as for or

as against the association it is written about. Its
message is the characteristically subjective and
impractical one, Do not be wholly indifferent to
this matter. But in the course of delivering it
Clough voices considerable dissatisfaction, not with
the forms of his country's government, but with the
spirit animating them. A governing class is essential and a plutocracy is essential, but the rich and
powerful are to refrain from manifesting their wealth
and their power in certain ways especially likely
to offend the lower classes,—and squeamish lookers-
on from the Universities—with the spectacle of
distressing contrasts in respect of happiness and
prosperity. So far as Clough had a political motive
for leaving Oxford, it seems fair to describe that
motive as a desire to gather up two huge and all
but exactly equal masses of evidence and reflection, one favourable and the other unfavourable
to Democracy, rather than to throw his own weight
into the fight on either side.

A strong impulse to change came to Clough through
his personal relations. His family, indeed, and
most of his friends advised him to stay where he
was. But in the year before, Matthew Arnold had
given up his Fellowship at Oriel to become secretary
to Lord Lansdowne, thereby at once setting Clough
an example of restlessness and making the college
a less pleasant place of residence for him. The
two were very close together at this time. In a
letter to his sister of March 1848, Arnold says of a

temptation to political writing which he had overcome, "So I desisted, and have only poured forth a little to Clough, we two agreeing like two lambs in a world of wolves." It was at this time, too, that Clough met Emerson. He writes to him first in November 1847, to ask him to visit him at Oxford. He is emboldened to do so, he states, by the fact that his sister has recently met Emerson in Liverpool. Emerson came to Oxford toward the end of the winter term, and spent three days. The two were much together in the following spring. They were in Paris at the same time, and dined together daily for a month, as Clough records in a letter to Thomas Arnold. Later they met frequently in London, and before he sailed for America in the middle of July, Emerson was with Clough at his home in Liverpool. " He gives you an impression," Clough writes, "of perfect intellectual cultivation." It is easy to suppose that Clough permitted or persuaded the older man to talk much to him of self-reliance and freedom from conventionality. Self-reliance Clough had been able to maintain at Oxford fairly well, but to live untrammelled by conventionality in that most conventional place in all the world was a vastly more difficult if not an utterly hopeless undertaking.

To be thoroughly of its decade this examination of motives would probably have begun as well as ended with an inquiry into the facts of the physical life of the subject. Some plausible explanations would doubtless be afforded by such an inquiry. At least two physical effects are obvious—a restless discontent proceeding from prolonged celibacy, and a weariness of the business of living resulting from the tubercular tendency to which Clough was finally to succumb. He really needed rest and change. This is proved, perhaps, by the gusto with which, conscientious man that he was, he idled away the pleasant months of his year of freedom.

Clough went to Paris on the 1st of May 1848, and remained there five weeks. Much was going on in Paris. These were the days of struggle between bourgeoisie and populace for the control of the newly formed republic. Clough looked on with delight at the *émeute* of the 15th May, and at the *fête* of the following Sunday. His letters show him sympathetic with the proletariat, though not so much in the manner of a genuine enthusiast for democracy as in that of the spectator at a game who chooses a side in order to sharpen his interest. " I am a bad hand at lionizing," he writes. " I do little else than potter about under the Tuileries chestnuts, *pour savourer la république*." This indeed was on the day before the rioting, and he admits to a considerable depression during the week that followed it. But there is a decided air of detachment about Clough's comments on the revolution— an absence of any indication that his feelings had been really stirred by it. What did arouse his enthusiasm was the strong sense of life itself, moving to whatever ends and by whatever rules, which he got from the stir of the boulevards.

Returning from France, he divided his summer between London and Liverpool. During the month of September he wrote his first long poem — *The Bothie of Tober-na-Vuolich*. He wrote it at his home in Liverpool—in a small room of an upper story, his sister says, of their small house in Vine Street, near Edge Hill. It was published by Macpherson, an Oxford bookseller, in November 1848, and reprinted in America, at Cambridge, in the following year.

At Oxford the poem was received with considerable interest, and on the whole with favour, but with a good deal of surprise. The Tractarian Movement had left Oxford in the habit of assuming that religion must be at the bottom of any sudden eccentricity in the actions of any of her sons, and that she would be presented duly with a full and solemn explanation of the eccentricity. This presumption was especially strong in the case of a man who bore the marks of inward struggle in his talk and appearance as obviously as Clough bore them. Hearing of a new book by him, Oxford went forth to buy a set of theological reasons for giving up a Fellowship, and was confused to find herself reading instead a humorous narrative poem so far from saintly that some of its lines struck her as decidedly *risqué*. Oxford really liked the book, however, whether on account of its local allusions, as Clough

himself suggests in a letter, or because it appealed
to a strong love of simple, open-air living that was
still there, although University poets and preachers
of the past generation had not allowed it expression.

Outside of Oxford *The Bothie* created no great
stir. It was reviewed scornfully by the *Spectator*,
and effusively by William Rossetti, in the first
number of the *Germ*. Much the most interesting
and important criticism of it was contributed by
Charles Kingsley to the January 1849 number of
Fraser's. Kingsley's first reason for liking the poem
is its freedom from the tone and accent of Tractarian-
ism. It is not " a sickly bantling of the Lyra
Apostolica school." He is enthusiastic about its
health and vigour and manliness. " There runs
through the poem a general honesty, a reverence for
facts and nature—a belief that if things are here,
they are here by God's will or the devil's, to be faced
manfully, and not to be blinked cowardly ; in short,
a true faith in God—which makes Mr. Clough's
poem, light as may seem the subject and the style,
and coming just now as it does from noble old Oxford,
anything but unimportant, because they indicate
a more genial and manly, and therefore a more
poetic and more godly spirit, than any verses which
have come out of Oxford for a long time past."
With this genuinely classical spirit, Kingsley finds,
the hexameter form is in admirable correspondence.
If the ridiculous is admitted alongside of the sub-
lime it is in wise deference to the real nature of a

world in which the two go always hand in hand.
Subject matter was novel, and it was right that
treatment should be novel. In short, Kingsley
said all that he could to encourage the sale of the
little book. His influence at this time, when his
first novel had not yet appeared, was not, of course,
nearly so great as it was to become.

Clough was greatly encouraged by the praise
his poem received, the more so as it did not commit
him to any serious pretensions as a poet, and as he
had written it very offhandedly and hastily. He
writes to Emerson in the winter that although he
started writing in September, he had no thought
of this or any other poem in July. Yet the experience out of which Clough developed his story was
an accumulation not of this but of the preceding
summer. In the long vacation of 1847 he had gone
to the Highlands as tutor of a reading party of
undergraduates. Among these, Thomas Arnold records, were Warde Hunt, later a Member of Parlia-
ment, and Charles Lloyd, the son of a bishop of
Oxford. Arnold himself, with John Campbell
Shairp, Theodore Walrond, and one or two others,
were making a walking tour through Scotland, and
turned aside to visit Clough and his party at Drumnadrochit, on the north shore of Lake Ness, where
they had settled down for several weeks in a large
farm-house. On the way thither, as both Arnold
and Shairp have told, they two left the others of
their party and walked north along the west side of

Loch Ericht. All the land here belonged to the
deer forest of Lord Abercorn, and there was no
human dwelling on all the shore except a forester's
hut, named on the maps " Toper-na-Fuosich."
This is the name Clough used at first for the title
of his poem. The two walkers were hospitably
received there and spent the night, and told Clough
of their pleasant experience when they met him at
Drumnadrochit. When his reading party broke
up he and a friend began a long ramble through
the Western Highlands by taking this walk along
Loch Ericht and stopping at the forester's hut.
Some of the incidents of *The Bothie*, according to
Shairp, happened to them while they were stopping
at an inn on Loch Rannoch ; and in Glenfinnan,
at the head of Loch Shiel, they ran into the ball
which Clough utilized—a celebration given by
MacDonald of Glen Aladale in honour of the officers
of some naval vessels then lying in a near-by port.
The high spirits of *The Bothie* are genuine enough
to show, without the testimony of Clough's friends,
how completely he enjoyed these things.

In order to fit a story to his scenes, his characters,
and his reflections, Clough centres attention on a
hero whom he calls Philip Hewson, a member of
the reading party, a radical and a poet, and of course
a lover. Hewson is partly Thomas Arnold, it has
been conjectured, but what is obviously truer is
that he, as well as the tutor, " the wise man Adam,"
is Clough. After the ball and the ensuing discus-

G

sions about ladies of high and low degree have disrupted the scholarly contentment of the reading party, Philip goes off by himself, to wander and to think. What he is thinking about is' mating—in connection first with pretty farmer's daughter Katie, then with Lady Maria, and last and resultfully with heroine Elspie, sensible daughter of the smith at Tober-na-Vuolich. Much of the poem, and of the best of it, is made up of the gay talk of the reading party, and is not very closely knit up with the story. Yet, perhaps because the whole piece is so informal, no absence of unity distresses the reader ; the idea that life must be lived soberly but can be lived happily at the same time, runs through all the talking and acting and, large and obvious as it sounds, seems to provide a perfectly adequate coherence.

The treatment of Oxford in the poem is, in a manner, indirect. Oxford is picked up from the valley of the Isis and set down in the Calvinistic and democratic Highlands. The contrast is a strong one, and adds to the variety and charm of the poem, though Clough minimizes it on the whole, his purpose being to discuss his problem as universal and not as particular. It is never a contrast between one side as good and the other as bad. In the end, it is true, Philip marries Elspie and takes her off to New Zealand—but, first, he goes back to the University and takes his degree. The University is the best possible place to train for life—it is emphatically not life itself. It is interesting to notice that all Clough's undergraduate characters are very different from what he had been as an undergraduate and from his ideals of that time. They all possess this sense which he had lacked, of real life as quite another kind of thing from Oxford. They are, indeed, almost that " rougher element " whose very existence Clough had deprecated in Rugby if not in Balliol days ; yet here he is at last, finding just in these health and sense and truth. Oxford is a place for young barbarians to play, Clough agrees—to work also, but much in the same play spirit. Youth had been right, after all, and the aged wisdom wrong which had too much impressed itself on the years when he ought to have been young.

Indeed the most interesting thing *The Bothie* shows about Clough is that he has entered at last upon his own belated boyhood. " As a boy," he says in one of his letters, " I had less of boyish enjoyment of any kind whatever, either at home or at school, than nine-tenths of boys ; certainly, even as a man I think I have earned myself some title to live for some little interval, I do not say in enjoyment, but without immediate devotion to particular objects : on matters, as it were, of business." He realizes, that is, that he is setting back the clock of his spirits, and is doing it, in part, deliberately. Yet the change bears every appearance of spontaneity, too. There is nothing disagreeably kittenish about *The Bothie*. He has not had to force this

new interest of his in visible and tangible persons
and things.   It is a yet keener interest than the old
one in invisibles.   It cannot be said to have held
steady throughout the remaining years of his life,
but it never failed him long, it made him definitely a
happy man, and in its first flowering it enabled him to
paint, in *The Bothie*, one of the most attractive pictures ever made of the Anglo-Saxon ideal of youth.

It was remarked in connection with Clough's
earlier religious poems that when at last he reached
a sort of resting place in the course of his arduous
quest for this kind of truth, he found his hard-won
position rather barren and unsatisfactory as a
basis for continued contemplation, but inspiriting
in so far as it led to action and to concern with concrete things.   Merely to think that action was the
thing was not, of course, satisfactory—or Clough's
life would have been a singularly satisfying experience.   It was needful for him to know that he was
absolutely acting.   The exhilaration of *The Bothie*
is best explicable by the circumstance that just at
the time he was writing it the feeling that he was
so acting ruled its author's breast.   Michaelmas
term was about to begin, and he for the first time
since his tenth year was not going back to school,
but was out in the world, once and for all, to
work and to live.   Later, the new course was to
discover obstacles as serious as those of the old,
and to induce the despair and the cynicism that
break out in *Dipsychus*.   But for the present all

is well. The world is brave and good, and from top to bottom there is nothing in it that cannot be looked at straight and steadily—nothing that so looked at will not increase the sum of courage and good cheer.

It has unfortunately a paradoxical sound to say of a book that it is at once thus optimistic, lighted up with the glamour of youth, and also singularly realistic. This may be said of *The Bothie*. It is high-spirited and not unromantic, but it bears at the same time every mark of an almost complete fidelity to Clough's experience. This closeness to actuality has brought upon it the charge that it is pedestrian and obvious. We celebrate the virtues of simplicity, correctness of observation, and omission of the irrelevant, and for the rare combination of them, when we find it, pedestrian and obvious are likely to be our words. The mystery Hewson saw in Elspie was not enough to add to beauty the proportion of strangeness which English readers required ; and it has occurred to Americans that the greater popularity the poem has had with them may possibly rest on their inferior acquaintance with the ways of Highland reading parties. Clough's persistent dread of the factitious was the conscious and volitional side of the freedom from the instinct to dream which, strangely for a poet, was natural to him. It prevented him from giving to the material any more than to the form of his work very much of what could seriously be called poetic elevation. But truth ages well, even when it is bald ; and the homely persons and real feelings of *The Bothie* have already outlasted many more decorative heroes and heroines of Victorian song, and much sentiment that was only almost true.

In spite of its hexameters it is not difficult to take *The Bothie* as a novel, and a decidedly realistic novel. As a photograph of mid-century Britons it is more truthful, not only than other poems, but also than the great professedly realistic novels of its day. There is less imagination in it, for better and for worse, and less illusion, than in *David Copperfield* or *The Newcomes*—less poetry, in a sense. The most important thing in life to Dickens is sympathy ; to Thackeray, it is honour ; but to Clough, it is work. Clough held his readers down to the inexorable reality they were so glad to escape through the humour of Dickens, or the sentiment of Thackeray, through long introspection with Tennyson, or through spasmodic bursts of bravery with Browning : he held them down to the central truth that man must work to live, and always under circumstances falling short, in some respect or other, of ideal dignity, and holding out, except in rare cases, no prospect of any adequate reward for the individual.

" Let us get on as we can, and do the thing we are fit for ;
Every one for himself, and the common success for us all, and
Thankful, if not for our own, why then for the triumph of others."

And the second concern of life, love, is best looked at in close association with work, not kept apart from its contamination. For Clough, and his Philip Hewson, what stirs the sentiment of chivalry in man is not the irresponsibility of a Dora, not the saintliness of an Agnes, not the fine ladyship and the charity of an Ethel Newcome, but the sight of

"some delicate woman
Serving him, toiling—for him, and the world ; some tenderest
    girl, not
Over-weighted, expectant, of him, is it ? "

Men are to learn, and to teach the other sex, that women are most beautiful when they are most useful.

" Bending with blue cotton gown skirted up over striped linsey-
    woolsey,
Milking the kine in the field, like Rachel, watering cattle,
Rachel, when at the well the predestined welcomed and kissed her,
Or, with pail upon head, like Dora beloved of Alexis,
Comely, with well-poised pail over neck arching soft to the
    shoulders,
Comely in gracefullest act, one arm uplifted to stay it,
Home from the river or pump moving stately and calm to the
    laundry ;
Ay, doing household work, which some one, after all, must do,
Needful, graceful therefore, as washing, cooking, and scouring,
Or, if you please, with the fork in the garden uprooting potatoes."

Nothing in *The Bothie* is more attractive than the mingled good sense and fineness of its attitude toward women. The discussion of the beauty of work for women is an echo presumably of Clough's long talks with his sister about what she was to do in the world. But since in the poem the tasks

Clough talks about for women are not the new, but the old tasks, the poem was not regarded at the time, nor can it be now, as a document of any importance in the woman movement. His thinking on the subject bore fruit rather through personal influence than through anything written. His sister, whose unusual character developed rather slowly, became in the decade after his death one of the persons most actively interested in the education of women. A considerable inheritance from the Perfect family gave her means and leisure to devote to the cause. With the Sidgwicks and others, she was a moving spirit in the establishment of a hall of residence for women at Cambridge, and in securing their admission to lectures and examinations. When Newnham Hall was founded, she was made its Principal, and she retained the position after the hall became a college—in all, for twenty years. She herself considered that the facts and the ideas which she worked with and which she passed on to many others, had come to her from her brother. A similar connection of Clough's with the enfranchisement of women may be found in the position he held as the trusted friend and adviser of Miss Florence Nightingale.

The difficulties of the morality of work as a message for poetry are, first that it is practical, and, second, that it is unescapable. It is capable of immediate and perfectly objective application. It almost commands the reader to drop his book.

It is the principle of life which everybody knows, and to evade the too pressing consciousness of which is for many readers the only reason for ever reading poetry at all. It calls for just the cheerful and steady and unassuming efforts that the reader is tired of putting forth, and calls for them by old names, with no promises held out to the instincts for novelty and drama. Nor does it offer the rest from strife, the sense of superiority, the indifference to fate, which Samuel Butler awards to the man who finds his level in life and travels ahead on it. The hero of *The Way of All Flesh* drops away from his old associates and thinks he has found the real truth about life in no longer trying to live up to their expectations of him, or to enthusiasms and ideals of his own, and in being content with easily attainable satisfactions. This is to take not merely an objective but a hand-to-mouth view of life, and considering the long record of human aspiration, a very inadequate view. The hero of *The Bothie* confines himself to attainable ideals, but these remain ideals none the less ; he is deliberately committing himself, therefore, to the wearing come-and-go of hope and disappointment which everybody sees life to be who is not putting some forced interpretation on it for the sake of his comfort. Clough's lust for sincerity did him several kinds of disservice, but one service it rendered was to enable him to describe a quite extraordinarily honest and balanced way of facing life, and so to make his work truly realistic, from the moral point of view as well as in respect to the portrayal of manners.

A simple way of proclaiming possession of the truth which Clough does not employ is the denunciation of shams. The tutor Adam does indeed persuade Hewson to distinguish between the Good and the Attractive, but they both see that these do not exist apart, but always in some degree of commingling. It is only the absolute idealist who can afford to denounce shams very heavily. Carlyle could do it, because even when he reached the inevitable conclusion that one thing in actual life is just as much a sham as another, he had his transcendental world left. He had the dreaming faculty, for which past and future are alive equally with the present in a vast romantic system created by the imagination. But Clough was no dreamer of dreams. Life interested him not as a thing to marvel at, but as a thing to control, or else to endure. It was not his practice to maintain an imaginary world wherein he could operate as toys of his mind notions of justice and symmetry which he found unrealized in the world of experience. Hence, whenever he destroyed anything for himself by calling it sham, his universe suffered a definite loss, which he had no means of making up. He could separate the good from what was attractive and from what was neither ; but he could not carry his classification to the point of marking off a class of gigmen or of barbarians as finally wrongheaded and negligible. He had to keep on hunting for good everywhere, and when he could not find it the only thing for him to do was to change his specifications of good. The hold of Carlyle, and of the German and the Platonic traditions is strong on him ; so that when he does his first thinking in this new way, which is his own way, he covers it up with a show of half-seriousness, and apologizes for it further with the sub-title, " A Long-Vacation Pastoral."

This lightness of touch in *The Bothie* seems to depend more than on anything else on the use of the hexameter form. In one of his letters to Emerson, Clough asks him to " convey to Mr. Longfellow the fact that it was a reading of his *Evangeline* aloud to my mother and sister, which, coming after a reperusal of the *Iliad*, occasioned this outbreak of hexameters." At this time and for more than ten years later there was much talk in England on the profound question whether there really was, or might be, any such thing as an English Hexameter. Clough's public had been educated, largely, through the scansion and the imitation of Virgil and Homer, and it found the easiest and most self-satisfying sort of attention to pay to the new poem in the perception of damning differences between *The Bothie* and the *Æneid*. These comparisons were not always wholly unfavourable, as witness the most widely read of them, Arnold's incidental disposal of Clough's supposed classical ambitions in his lecture On *Translating Homer* : " Mr. Clough's hexameters are excessively, needlessly rough ; still, owing to the native rapidity of this measure, and to the directness of style which so well allies itself with it, his composition produces a sense in the reader which Homer's composition also produces—the sense of having, within short limits of time, a large portion of human life presented to him, instead of a small portion." But generally it was held against Clough, either that he should have attempted hexameters at all, or else that he should have afforded more evidence of an unflagging effort to deviate in no single respect from the classical models.

At a time when so much of the verse we read professes nothing less than complete freedom, the seriousness with which we take this sort of criticism is lightened. A majority of ears are not greatly offended, are even somewhat agreeably titillated, by Clough's gambolling measures. He seems at home in the form he has chosen, and able to speak his mind freely in it, both in gay and in sober mood. Besides, there is special fitness in a classical measure as a medium for a man who has spent his life reading and teaching the classics, as also in his taking with this medium, since it is " shop " to him, great and frivolous liberties. A mind so academic as Clough's was certain to betray itself sooner or later in any case, and to be mock-academic from the start was a good way to obviate self-criticism on this score in the act of composition, as well as to forestall some of

could surely be made a useful link between the liveliness of the football-field and the dancing-room on the one hand, and on the other the remoteness— at times, possibly, even dullness—of the study of literature.

CHAPTER VI

AMOURS DE VOYAGE

IN the autumn after he gave up his fellowship Clough returned to Oxford for a stay of several weeks. Professor Conington tells of finding him in some small and cheap lodgings in Holywell, living without fire in cold weather. The rooms were near Parson's Pleasure, the University bathing place, and Clough's soul seems to have demanded for its good a November series of daily plunges. Later in the winter he spent most of his time in Liverpool with his mother and sisters. He did not remain long without the certainty of employment for the next year. He was offered and accepted the Headship of University Hall, an institution which furnished tuition and living accommodations to students attending lectures in University College, London. This was the non-sectarian half of London University. It was understood to be rather glad to get hold of Clough ; and Clough on the whole rejoiced in his appointment, though he confesses in a letter written just after receiving it that he has his misgivings. He had landed, at any rate, in one of a very few places congenial to his way of being quite religious without either affirming or denying much of anything. He writes to the reverend authority with whom his negotiations had been made that he has attended various sorts of service with complete tolerance, that he prefers Westminster Abbey to a Scotch chapel, and that his dislike of the Thirty-nine Articles is firm. He will strongly approve of prayers, but will not superintend them, nor even promise faithful attendance. He will not proselytize, because he has nothing to proselytize to ; but he will not keep absolute silence. His employers found nothing to object to in this statement of principles.

In April of 1849 he went to Rome. There, as in Paris the year before, he was present at an interesting time. The new Pope, after attempting a compromise with the revolutionary spirit, had fled the city in disguise, and Mazzini with his associated triumvirs was in command. The Republica Romana had endured for two months. Garibaldi was at hand to defend it against the French force of invasion under General Oudinot. The eyes of Europe were on the eternal city ; and they remained on it until, at the end of July, the reinforced French army was finally successful in its singular purpose of overthrowing a sister republic and restoring the absolute rule of the Pope. Throughout these exciting months Clough remained in Rome, imprisoned in it for most of the time by the vicissitudes of war. His letters show him unalarmed at the situation, alive to the hurry of events and the personalities of the actors great and small, not very clear, excusably enough, as to the significance of the turmoil, and not much inclined to proceed to conclusions about liberty and democracy and popular wrongs. He meets Mazzini, and finds him practical and even shifty. After the victories in May he is enthusiastic enough to speak of the "wonderful courage and glorious generosity" that the republic has shown under Mazzini's inspiration. Later it is not hard for him to see a general apathy in the Romans ; and when he leaves Italy it is with the exclamation : " Farewell, politics, utterly ! What can I do ? Study is much more to the purpose."

The holiday concluded in this serious and rather pessimistic frame of mind was from the first, apparently, a more sober and reflective and a less joyous affair than the earlier vacation journeys to the Highlands and to Paris. Clough is an unfriendly critic in nearly all that he writes about Rome and the Romans. He lets himself be seen as the standard English traveller, with the one inclusive grievance that all things everywhere are not modelled with sufficient accuracy upon the authoritative English usage. Possibly the heat, and attendant circumstances, of a Roman summer affected him physically. He says nothing of his health in his letters ; but he was never at any time given to complaining. At any rate, the long poem which he wrote during this vacation and immediately after it is quite devoid of the exuberance of *The Bothie*. The freedom and

the carelessness of writing of *The Bothie* were real and
not pretended ; but *Amours de Voyage* shows in
every line that its author was willing to spend time
on polishing, if not that he was adept at polishing.
And greater still is the difference in emotional tone,
a difference sufficiently indicated on the title pages :
the *Amours de Voyage* is so far from announcing itself as a " Vacation Pastoral " that it starts off with
a number of most dispiriting quotations, one of them
Shakespeare's :

> " Oh, you are sick of self-love, Malvolio,
>   And taste with a distempered appetite ! "

and another the still more disquieting line from a
French novel :

> " Il doutait de tout, même de l'amour."

The Clough of the *Amours*, whether because of the
weather, or his health, or an astonishing surmise
concerning the public taste, or merely the attainment of a stage in the orderly process of his life's
thinking, is very much in doubt, not merely concerning love itself, but even concerning virtue itself.

This pervading doubt extended to Clough's estima-
tion of the value of his poem after he had written it.
He had rushed into print with *The Bothie,* and in the
early part of the year 1849 had published his short
poems in the volume called *Ambarvalia*, for which
he and his school friend, the Reverend Thomas
Burbidge, shared responsibility. But he kept the
Amours de Voyage by him for nine years. He sold
it at last to James Russell Lowell for the *Atlantic*

Monthly, where it ran through the numbers from February to May of 1858. It was reprinted in 1862, the year after Clough's death. The money he received from the *Atlantic Monthly*, " a handsome sum," he writes to a friend, was the only money Clough ever got out of his poetry.

A letter which Clough wrote to Palgrave in the winter after his return from Italy shows that his suspicions of his new work were of its manner rather than its matter. He has sent Palgrave the manuscript to read and has asked for criticisms, and is replying to a letter containing some which he complains of as " not half trenchant enough." And they are not quite to the point. " What I want assurance of," he writes, " is in the way of execution rather than conception. If I were only half as sure of the bearableness of the former as I am of the propriety of the latter, I would publish at once." It would be interesting to know certainly just what Clough feared was the matter with his lines. In the opinion of most, or all, of his critics, what ails them is that though unobjectionable they are plain. But plain is precisely what Clough was convinced verse ought to be. It is in this poem that the line occurs which is more frequently quoted than any other of his :

" . . . the horrible pleasure of pleasing inferior people."

To remain unpolluted by that pleasure seems to have been his first principle of composition. He was afraid, we may suppose, that Palgrave would point out to him passages proffering inferior varieties of pleasure—appealing by tinkling melody to the kind of people who read Tom Moore, or by over-luxuriant imagery to the less discriminating of the admirers of Tennyson, or by clatter and dash to friends of the *Lays of Ancient Rome*. But unfortunately not Palgrave nor any one could possibly bring these charges. The hexameters of the *Amours* are never irregular and slipshod as are some of those of *The Bothie*, and they are not garrulous, nor gushing, nor sing-song. There are, in fact, very many bad things which they are not, and the sole difficulty remains that there are so few good things which they are.

However far Clough may have been from seeing where his faults of style lay, he was right in turning his attention toward them at last, and in permitting himself meanwhile some confidence in the soundness of his views of life. It was too late for any degree of concern about form to enable him to write one of the superlatively beautiful poems of the century ; but his new painstaking established *Amours de Voyage* as much the most finished, most nearly perfect, of his own works. His style at any rate did not stand in his way. It did not prevent him from expressing with clearness and brevity a full and complicated and a very knowing set of ideas. Since there is not much passion in the poem, no vivid action, and very little natural description, it had little occasion to rise to any impressive height. The lines that a reader

retains in mind are likely to owe their persistence
to an adequacy of candour rather than to any more
brilliant quality.   They are such lines as these :

" If there is any one thing in the world to preclude all kindness,
  It is the need of it—it is this sad, self-defeating dependence."

It is much truer of the *Amours* than of *The Bothie*
that whether it is a poem or not it is certainly a novel.
It is a careful study of manners and motives, and it
is not simple, sensuous, and impassioned. But to
any who would proceed from this to a conclusion
that the form of the work was a mistake, the fact
that it does somehow attain artistic integrity ought
to be clear enough to provide a measure of restraint.
It does not crystallize any part of the beauty of life
very clearly ; but it gives a strong and an integral
impression of beauty as always just out of reach.
And it is an irritating work ; but it is full of honest
thinking.

As in his earlier poem, Clough enlarges but little
on his own experience in making his plot. His
hero is in most respects in just the situation that he
himself is in at the time of writing : in Rome, doing
the sights and looking on at the efforts of the citizens
to keep out the French besiegers. But Claude, the
hero, has a third interest in life—falling in love ; and
it is here tha this creator calls on his imagination.
There is no reason to suppose Clough had any sentimental experiences in Rome. In the letter to Palgrave, already referred to, he as much as says
that he had none. " Gott and Teufel ! my friend,"

he exclaims, " you don't suppose all that comes from myself ! I assure you it is extremely *not* so." Since the other two of the three elements of his content do obviously come from himself, it must be the love story that he is talking about. It is a quite simple love story, besides—not at all out of the range even of Clough's very cautious imagination. It provides, of course, the central thread, with the story of the siege and the comments on antiquities furnishing an apt and undistracting series of digressions, pretty closely woven into the general scheme. The poem is made up of letters, most of them written by Claude to his confidant ; and if he had talked of only one subject in these letters he would be open to praise for single-ness of purpose, and his love story would have been something very different from this record of uncertainty and hesitation.

Clough's tourist's observations on Rome are partly æsthetic and partly religious, and he is very much more at home in the latter kind of talk than in the former. He seems to mean his hero to be taken as something of a connoisseur, as a man whose weariness of the world is largely explained by his having attended too much to the mere beauty of it. But the remarks he attributes to his Claude—that the Coliseum is merely large, St. Peter's full of sculptures, and Rome itself " rubbishy "—are better understandable as the comments of a man with a little knowledge of jargon, and with good intentions, but not necessarily with any sense at all of architectural and sculptural beauty.

He boasts, this Claude, of hating Childe Harold ; but his words offer no justification, except of the coldest *nil admirari* sort for his feeling superior to it. His distastes, in short, are so pettish as to cause him to fall short of the minimum of dignity desirable in a hero of a poem of this sort and length. His religious dislikes are more vigorously expressed than his artistic dislikes and seem somewhat honester. But the note of passion here is a little bewildering. It is unnatural to Clough, and unnatural to the tone of this work to write :

" these vile, tyrannous Spaniards,
These are here still —how long, O ye heavens, in the country of Dante ?
These, that fanaticised Europe, which now can forget them."

Other reflections on Church history are more tolerant and more attractive. But on the whole the reader is glad when the activities of the siege close the museum to Claude, and turn his attention away from the churches and toward the crowds in the streets.

One of the things Arnold says about Clough in the eulogy of him at the end of the lectures *On Translating Homer* is that he had a single-hearted care for his object of study. Arnold certainly meant the phrase as a compliment ; but it can be taken as expressive of the chief inferiority of Clough to himself. Clough was indeed zealous enough about seeing his object as it in itself really was to satisfy Arnold or any one. But he stopped with the seeing. He did not, as Arnold did, have two things in his mind and heart, one of them his object of study and the other the collective intelligence, such as it was, of his countrymen ; he was not continually searching his object of study for ways in which he might raise the level of that intelligence. He was inclined to be too little aware of things as becoming, and too neglectful of his opportunities for assisting in the general process. He had something of Bacon's faith, that things if once rightly seen could be counted on to produce new things, new truths ; he did not see the need of investigating with a specific, practical purpose, nor the need of forming hypotheses and doing his best by them. All this can be seen in the way he treats the stand of the Roman Republicans. Arnold would have felt just as superior to them, at most points, as Clough felt. But he would have been sure to find at least one lucid and striking lesson which the English could learn from them. Clough is content to set down what he sees and what he feels, and perhaps one or two more old truths which he considers to have been disproved. And he lets it go at that. On public affairs he is an impression-ist ; and his impressions always lack novelty, and sometimes lack vividness.

The best thing about Clough's handling of the siege is the perfect candour with which he describes the feelings it moved in him ; and a similar merit is the photographic accuracy of his pictures of what went on in the streets. Claude is much less vain than the usual hero of this type and of this century.

He does not try to make virtues, nor on the other hand grandiose sins, of his emotional peculiarities. He is now enthusiastic, and now apathetic, about the Roman defence, and he does not try to make out any sort of consistency for his moods. He admits that he himself feels no call to fight for liberty, and does not, in a more modern fashion, arrogate his reluctance as a point of superiority :

" Sweet it may be and decorous, perhaps, for the country to die ; but
  On the whole, we conclude the Romans won't do it, and I shan't."

Very observant, and frightfully cynical for the middle of the century, though sincere enough in present light, are these lines :

" Victory ! Victory ! Victory !—Ah, but it is, believe me,
Easier, easier far, to intone the chant of the martyr
Than to indite any pæan of any victory. Death may
Sometimes be noble ; but life, at the best, will appear an illusion.
While the great pain is upon us, it is great ; when it is over
Why, it is over. The smoke of the sacrifice rises to heaven
Of a sweet savour, no doubt, to Somebody ; but on the altar
Lo, there is nothing remaining but ashes and dirt and ill odour."

Clough turns his historical background to good account : it provides vivid activity to contrast with Claude's languor, and it gives opportunities for Claude to bring himself out in denials of the utility of action, and refusals to sympathize with it.

The love story is of a type that is common enough in life, but exceedingly rare in fiction. The public likes its love to run a smooth course. It also likes it now

and then to run over the edge of a precipice or into
the mouth of a fiery furnace. It does not like it to
run up and down sand dunes until it finally loses itself
in the waste. The honest Clough was convinced that
the course of love was frequently of this last sort.
He was looking, we may suppose, into his own heart,
and finding there reason to fear that any love he
himself might contract would be likely to take this
desolate middle way between tragedy and bliss. It
may have been part of his calculation that, inferior
people having always preferred one extreme or the
other, superior persons might be attracted by the
mean. And for that calculation a good deal could
be said. And much can be said for Clough's story.
It moves disappointingly to a disappointing end; but
it could not possibly end in another way, for the
thesis of it is that love and lovers are often disappointing. Having once undertaken an ungrateful
task, Clough at least executes it faithfully.

The hero is an idler, and more fashionable and
more epicurean Clough—on the whole, considerably
different. The exigencies of living in a besieged city
throw him into some unusually familiar contacts,
especially with a prosperous family of English business people, the Trevellyns. He finds himself
attracted particularly to one of the daughters, Mary.
The attraction is strong, and grows stronger. But
like everything else that concerns his own being
intimately, it receives from him a vast expenditure
of thought. It becomes translated into ideas, and

this form of it persists alongside of the original emotional impulse. And as idea it is startlingly weaker than as impulse. Claude's nature compels him to attend to it in its intellectual form. He has to reflect for the thousandth and ten thousandth times that Mary is less polished than many another girl, that her beauty though unquestioned is not at all unusual, that her family is the family of a country banker, and that she probably does not like him. While he is reflecting, the Trevellyns leave Rome, Mary reluctantly and hopefully. Claude's mind being thus made up for him by deprivation, he starts in pursuit. But a series of delays and failures to meet produces a reversion to indecisiveness. And there the story ends.

The letter method of writing the story was suggested perhaps by Werther. It has the advantage of lending itself to the most uninterrupted flow of introspection. And Claude is yet more introspective than Werther, for Claude is worried about his ideas as well as about his feelings. Werther, Amiel, De Musset, Manfred, the hero of *Locksley Hall*—they may be ranked together in a contingent of fighters against themselves, with Hamlet as their captain. In order to keep the numbers of the band within reasonable limits, Russians may be excluded. It is so far a homogeneous collection that all its members have in common three things : sadness, weakness of will, and extreme self-consciousness. The first two are, alas, not very distinguishing traits, and it is the last that really sets these young men apart from their kind. But to call them all self-conscious is still not to deny that there may exist among them enormous differences. Clough's hero differs from all the rest in that he is much less sensitive than any of them. He is only half sensitive : he has plenty of moral and intellectual sensitiveness, but he is hardly above ordinary in respect of æsthetic and emotional sensitiveness. Clough could not endow his Claude with passion and with an acute sense of beauty because he lacked these himself. For the popularity of his poem this is a desperate want : it is for their passionateness and their keenness of perception that Hamlet and Werther have been loved. It is a poor compensation that Claude, the truer to his age, the better Victorian, and the better sensitive Victorian, for that his sensitiveness is thus limited.

The problem with which Clough poses his hero may be regarded as the second stage in a problem of Clough's own. He had worked out the first stage of it in *The Bothie*. He had become interested, rather late, and in his serious and unimpulsive way, in love. First there is the question of the woman, and that is talked over thoroughly by the reading party in the Highlands. And then, having thus provided himself with a theory of selection, it remains for Clough to understand and to explain to himself how he is to work up a meet degree of enthusiasm for a young woman once he has selected her.

He is moral idealist enough to desire that there should be no reserves, no weak spots, in his loyalty to her. He does not see that because his idealism is wholly of the moral kind he will never be capable of believing any one woman to be immensely superior to all others.   His love will never be blind.   He has a premonition of this, and it conflicts with his desire to love without any consciousness of defect. All this is anticipatory of the actual finding of the lady and resolving to win her.   Yet it would be wrong to think that the spirit in which Clough approached the matter was a scientific, or a pedantic, or a coldly calculating spirit.   These are byways that it must ever be difficult to keep out of in thinking about love apart from a specific object of love ; but Clough had such cleanness and reverence in him as enabled him to keep out of them as well as any man could. The finding of a mate filled his mind before it filled his heart.   But his thinking about it was as earnest as feeling would have been if feeling had happened to precede.

How to fall in love ?   Where to find the side of the angels in politics ?   Whether to fight for other people's womenfolk ?   How to avoid loneliness ?— here are obstacles enough to the straightforward living of the objective life that is made to seem so simple a matter in *The Bothie*. Clough is feeling himself baffled, obviously.   On account of his bafflement he belabours himself, in the person of Claude, for weakness of will.   He goes too far in his self-abasement, and makes Claude a poor creature, which he did not intend to do. " I have no intention of sticking up for him," he writes to Palgrave, " but certainly I did not mean him to go off into mere prostration and defeat." Yet to prostration and defeat the reader feels that this unfortunate hero goes. And readers and critics have gone on to take Clough as equally weak of will with his creation. But this is to misrepresent Clough sadly. Claude is not Clough—nor even, as he seemed to his creator, one-half of a dual Clough. It was imagination that Clough lacked, not will. Things to do did not readily present themselves to him ; but at nearly all times in his life he is perfectly competent to initiate and to persist in a difficult course of action, once he has become aware of it as desirable. All his friends admired him for his ability to make rules for himself and stand by them. He was more than usually hesitant, naturally, in a year in which the routine of his life was interrupted. But the man who had persistence enough to translate Plutarch and boldness enough to leave Oxford and to seek his fortune in America, was no Claude.

Amours de Voyage is at once Clough's most carefully wrought poem and the one in which he most clearly betrays his limitations. If he be assumed to have betrayed them to himself also, an explanation is provided for his letting the work go unpublished so long a time. He dares comparison in the *Amours* with Shakespeare and with Goethe, and these are

comparisons that he cannot endure.   Perhaps he did
not mean Claude to be a thorough-going idealist.
But he makes him too much of one to save him
from the fatal contrast. Claude is a refined and
intelligent young man, but he is a dwarf in the line
with Werther and Faust and Hamlet.   His tragedy
is their tragedy—that the gulf between desire and
reality cannot be bridged.   But the gulf in his case
is not magnificently wide.   His desire has not been
of the godlike strength to create for him a vision
of such a world as that which Hamlet saw, or Werther.
These won their stature by living in the imagined
world and adapting themselves to it until they were all
but fit to inhabit it in their real shapes.   With Claude
and with Clough, even the height of youth though
pure and noble had been earthly.   And so Claude
lacks the charm which alone can make a hero out
of another kind of man than the man of action, and
a more satisfactory hero, in art, than the man of
action can ever be.   Clough is not to be accused of
failing to realize something of this ; but realizing
it he should have seen—perhaps did see, too late—
that to create Claude was to create a character true
enough, indeed, but unattractive, uninspiring, and
unprofitable.

CHAPTER VII

DIPSYCHUS

TO Clough as to Dante the crisis of life came *nel mezzo del cammin.* He wrote his three long poems in three successive years, the thirtieth, thirty-first, and thirty-second of his life. The last of the three, *Dipsychus*, was written by a man older than the author of the first of them by much more than two years. *The Bothie*, of 1848, is a poem of youth and illusion ; *Dipsychus*, of 1850, is a work of disillusionment and maturity. And that *Dipsychus* was left unfinished may be taken to symbolize an issuance from the crisis that was not wholly victorious : that left Clough strengthened for the living out of his own life, indeed, but lamed for the pursuit of the poet's vocation of guiding the lives of others. In the rest of his life as in the years he had lived, repression was to be stronger than expression, and the prudent and responsible member of society stronger than the artist.

Like the works of the two preceding years, *Dipsychus* is the product of a vacation—though it is far from being written in a holiday spirit. When he wrote it, or started to write it, Clough was at the end of his first year of residence in London as Head of University

Hall.   It had not been a happy year.   Clough had felt lonely and insecure, and dissatisfied with the conditions and the prospects of his new work.   He had been finding his mind turned in upon itself not less than at Oxford, as he had so greatly hoped, but more.   The few letters that are preserved from this year are mostly taken up with moralizing.   The morals are of an exceptionally sound and healthy type ; and the indication from this as to the moralizer is, of course, that his desire, and so his lack also, of health of mind were exceptional.   " There is a great blessing, I sometimes think," Clough writes to Thomas Arnold, "in being set down amongst uncongenial people." And from this we may know that Clough's usual opinion of being set down amongst such people was that it was anything but a blessing.   " Let us not sit in a corner and mope," he urges in the same letter ; and there is the evidence of the *Memoir* that at this time " he became depressed and reserved to a degree quite unusual with him both before and afterwards."   It was the worst year of his life.   In a letter of May 1851 he writes : " Nothing is very good anywhere, I am afraid.   I could have gone cracked last year with one thing or another, I think, but the wheel comes round."

Doubtless Clough hoped to help the wheel come round when he took his vacation trip to Venice.   The journey was hasty, taken at the end of the summer, and no such letters survive to record it as those which recount the earlier and more cheerful visits to Paris and to Rome. The only lasting result of it is *Dipsychus*, and great as the merits of *Dipsychus*, are there is nothing in it to indicate that its author was incapable, or was even growing less capable, of " going cracked." It reveals a Clough who has reverted from the healthy objectivity of *The Bothie* to the old habit of tormenting himself with doubts : only now the torment is more critical, and fiercer. The mind, like the body, creates its anti-toxins, and Clough found himself possessed at this time of need with a priceless new agent—irony. But that greatest of curative resources, an interest in life round about, had departed from him. Travel, even in Italy, was not enough to bring it back. Local colour, rich in *The Bothie* and *Amours de Voyage*, in *Dipsychus* scarcely goes beyond the bare mention of various " points of interest " in Venice as the scenes of the hero's successive conversations with himself ; the gondola scene is an exception, but the stage-direction for any of the others might have been the Nevsky Prospekt as well as The Piazza, and the Bois de Boulogne as well as The Public Garden. Clough cannot possibly have enjoyed his journey. Perhaps he was not particularly fond of the poem that grew out of it. He did not publish it in his lifetime, nor talk much about it. Charles Eliot Norton included a great part of it in a contribution to the *North American Review* six years after Clough's death. It was first printed in the collected works in 1869.

Dipsychus is less attractive than the two other

long poems, and probably less read. They are about love, and *Dipsychus* about the much less poetical subject of work. Brave dreams are more likely to arise from speculation at the age of twenty than at thirty on the subject of what to do in the world. But *Dipsychus* is the most thoughtful and honest and intense and outspoken of the three. Few poems of anything like its length are so naïve. Clough is revealing the state of his innermost mind, directly, without any symbols or puppets or analogies. If the revelations do not immediately strike a reader as intimate, it is because they are so little sensational. It would be going too far, perhaps, to say confidently that they are not confessions because Clough has nothing to confess ; but certainly his life has been one of plain living and high thinking to a very unusual degree. It was possible, therefore, for his self-revelation to be as complete as Rousseau's without possessing any of that naturalistic and scandalous familiarity which a sort of universal pessimism is likely to take as the proof of Rousseau's or any man's veracity concerning the facts of his life. *Dipsychus* is the best possible answer to the careless acceptance of " mid-Victorian " as a synonym for hypocritical. It will show, to any but an exceptionally superficial or an exceptionally subtle cynic, high scruples surviving unimpaired by a most rigorous and clear-eyed process of undeception of self.

Also, formless as it is as a whole, *Dipsychus* has real poetry in it. Clough and his friends agree that

there was ordinarily something about him that was
cold and sluggish.   Even in the days of his intensest
religious feeling he did not get excited to the point
of nervousness.   But the unhappiness and the uncertainty that culminated in the summer of 1850
brought him then at last an alertness and agility
of nerves and mind quite foreign to the stateliness
and the inertia of his way of thinking before and
after that time.   His writing becomes rapid, and
strongly rhythmical.   It acquires a swing :

> " ' There is no God,' the wicked saith,
>   ' And truly it's a blessing,
> For what He might have done with us
>   It's better only guessing.' "

Several measures are used, and though there is a
plainness about all the verses, a number of them are
likely to stick in any memory :

> " How light we go, how soft we skim,
>   And all in moonlight seem to swim !
> The south side rises o'er our bark
> A wall impenetrably dark ;
> The north is seen profusely bright ;
> The water, is it shade or light ?
> Say, gentle moon, which conquers now !—
> The flood, those massy hulls, or thou ?
> (How light we go, how softly !   Ah,
> Were life but as the gondola ! "

Clough's is still an inadequate ear for a poet ; but it
is better than it has been.

Clough employs the dramatic form for his poem,
but he provides no drama.   There are but the two
figures, the hero and his projected questioning self,

the first denoted as Dipsychus and the second as the Spirit.   These go together about Venice, ostensibly to see the sights, and whenever they come to a place with a well-known name they are stopped and set at conversing.   Always the subject of the conversation is the same : Whether to remain aloof from the world and preserve ideal dignity, or to drop down into it and secure the relief of being like other people. Nothing happens ; and no deceptive hint is thrown out that anything ever will happen.   One feels that Dipsychus is on the losing side in the argument, and one gathers at the end that he has lost.   But the steps in such a contention need to be marked and pointed by events and changes of situation in order to be really effective in a work intended to be poetic, let alone dramatic.   And these events and changes Clough is too single-mindedly interested in his problem itself to supply.   Without them the division into scenes and the bald stage-directions " In St. Mark's," " At Torcello," etc., are scarcely even tantalizing—merely irritating.   All this is bad as art but good as truth concerning one human soul ; and the poem's lack of dramatic value may be taken as positively increasing its moral value, and especially its historical value as a record of the workings of a typical nineteenth-century mind.

This lack of dramatic value is so complete as to make *Dipsychus* one of the oddities of literature. No work of William Blake's exhibits a more thorough neglect of the desires and habits of the reading public. Dipsychus is discovered in the first scene scolding himself for his preoccupation with the ideas of a poem he has written the year before—Clough's *Easter Day, Naples,* 1849. His attendant ridicules him, and urges him to eschew anxiety and enjoy the passing hour. Next, the two are in the Public Garden ; and Dipsychus from fearing there is no God has taken to fearing that his motive in coming to Venice was the vulgar one of fearing (again) to be behind the times. They go to the hotel, where the Spirit lectures his slave on the advantages of society. In the next scene occurs all that can be called action in the work. The hero is jostled by an Austrian officer, who blames him for the collision and tells him to " get out." The thing has already happened when the scene opens, and the meagre account of it comes out only incidentally in the disquisition as to what Dipsychus will do about it. No reader could be so simple as to suppose there was ever any least chance that Dipsychus would do anything about it. So it goes—one talk after another until the final scene, in which Dipsychus pettishly tells his tempter :

> " So your poor bargain take, my man,
> And make the best of it you can."

Then follows an Epilogue, in prose, in which the poet and an uncle of his are represented, the one as condemning the poem directly and completely, the other as damning it, in defence, with the faintest of praise. After the Epilogue is printed *Dipsychus Continued*, *A Fragment.* In this there are three scenes ; and the

time of them is thirty years after the conclusion of Part
I. The action—and there really is a certain amount
of action here, at last—takes place in London. The
two-souled hero has come to be a distinguished judge.
A woman comes to see him in his study, and reproves
him for an entanglement they two had got into
thirty years before. She tells him her name was
formerly Pleasure and now is Guilt. Something in
that change of name, inadequately explained, has
with the aged Dipsychus the force of an awful revelation. He resigns the Lord Chief Justiceship, and it
is noised about by " Barristers " in the second scene
that he is dying. He does not die before he has
taken up another scene with his favourite activity
of soliloquizing on the very subjects he least likes
to think about. When the scene breaks off abruptly
and the poem ends, he has still done nothing so concrete and practical as to die. The reader wonders
how Clough refrained from the opportunity that
was his alone to provide a violent, discreditable, and
safely final ending for this most vexatious of heroes.

Dipsychus is constructed on a thought plot rather
than an action plot. But the thought plot also is
lacking in orderliness. Stages of progress go un-
marked. The central difficulty is that Dipsychus
reluctantly and passively allows truth to drive him,
instead of going out boldly to find truth. It is a
conflict of attrition. A temperament is arrayed
against facts, and refusing to take the offensive is
worn down until it makes a sudden submission, still

not decisively, but with reserves and backward glances. The factual world speaks against Dipsychus in the voice of "The Spirit." This Spirit considers it unimportant to make clear just who he is. Cosmocrator is the one of his many titles he seems most to approve ; and he has no quarrel with the final appellation Dipsychus bestows on him :

"The Power of this World ! hateful unto God."

He is Environment, summoning a lethargic human soul to free its energies and express itself in the only way in which soul can express itself, in action. And the soul objects that such expression involves mingling with matter, and so losing its purity. It is a soul of such muddy metal that it cannot be brought to want to express itself, but only to see that, in the light of the wisdom of the past, self-expression is a duty and is salvation. Dipsychus is breaking away from old things, not because he has exhausted their benefits and is yearning for new things, but because the old things have become absolutely intolerable, and the new, in spite of a repellent appearance, may not be positively less disagreeable. This is to put the moral conflict, everybody's conflict, into a form not only too abstract to be dramatic, but, merely as argument, too general to be novel, and too passive to be stimulating. A good train of narrative might have satisfied all these objections. Never did a work of art stand in greater need of a story. It was a particularly perverse stroke of Clough's fate which kept him from using a little of the creditable skill at narration which he discloses in *Amours de Voyage* and *Mari Magno* in the writing of *Dipsychus*.

This, with all its shortcomings, is the poem which has been called the English *Faust*. Clough himself, who risked the comparison, must have seen how disastrous it was to himself. Drama, the colour of life, movement, wealth of character, orderly development of idea—all the great qualities *Dipsychus* lacks, *Faust* possesses. The English work is a skeleton by the side of the German. It originated, of course, in a much slighter set of intentions. *Faust* is the work of a lifetime, *Dipsychus* of a season. Goethe selected widely separated intervals of exceptional spiritual health for working on his masterpiece; Clough's writing was done in a temporary fit of very serious and depressing anxiety concerning his future. This has much to do with another very great difference between the two poems : that *Faust* is universal, and *Dipsychus* is narrowly limited. In the mind of the one writer his symbols adapted themselves at different times to a great range of different aspects of the problem of life ; so they secure an adaptability which in the minds of readers can be carried still farther. But the mind of the other poet was intent on one problem throughout, and considered it in literal terms, of no general applicability. Hence everybody can see himself, and see humanity generally, in *Faust* ; but only the narrow class of self-tormentors can see themselves in *Dipsychus*. The most obvious of all the superiorities of the German poem is that its hero is so much greater a man than the leading figure of the English work. He is greater because he has tremendously more energy. He can meet life, survive its blows, and master it ; and *Dipsychus Continued* does not fool us into thinking that there was ever force enough in Clough's creature to enable him to attain a Lord Chief Justiceship or any other of the prizes for vigorous and successful living. Both heroes were dreamers, but the Englishman had no really great vision. Peace and piety were the only conditions of life that really attracted him ; he admits work, action, to a place among his ideals without any enthusiasm for it, and without any appreciation of what the joys of action really are. Clough was not egotist enough ever to think confidently of himself as doing widely effective things with his own life ; and the rule held in his case that man cannot conceive a character very much superior to himself at his best.

There are, perhaps, a few compensatory advantages on the side of *Dipsychus*. One has already been suggested—absence not merely of melodrama, but of drama, may be taken as a point of superiority in an attempt to represent the essential conflict of life just exactly as it really is. Truth may be there none the less for its failure to become apparent to minds accustomed to think of life as dramatic. And *Faust* is not merely dramatic, but very theatrical—written with the demands of the stage most prominently in mind ; whereas if Clough ever saw a play in all his life, he at any rate never makes mention of the fact in any of his letters or other writings. Yet he seems to have thought he could write a play ; and the completely undramatic nature of his effort as it stands may be largely due to the accident of failure to carry through the work as designed. The fragment of *Dipsychus Continued* suggests that Clough intended to furnish some sort of Venetian Gretchen to attract his hero in intervals between soliloquies. One feels that the world suffered no great deprivation of knowledge of things as they are when Clough thus held his hand from delineating such a daughter of Venice as he could represent saying thirty years later that her name was Guilt, and had once been Pleasure. Doubtless Clough would have claimed sympathy with such a type ; but how much real and effective sympathy had he ever at this time given himself occasion for feeling toward any one outside his own academic circle of life ? He is far behind Goethe in experience. From this inferiority also it is possible, casuistically perhaps, to make out for Clough's poem an advantage in the comparison. The principal reason why Clough's experience was poorer was that he had long had to confront the problem of making a living, as the Frankfort patrician never in his life had to confront it. This is but another angle of approach to the greater realism claimed for the English poem. The homeliness and indignity of work were well concealed from Goethe by the ceremony and the distinction of his position at a sovereign, though tiny, court. Work under such conditions was not the matter of enduring and submitting that it is for most men. But what it is for most men it was for Clough. He is with Hardy and with many another in believing that as years and centuries pass living will be seen as enduring, more and more. Such a trend would be anything but unfavourable to the reputation of *Dipsychus*.

It is interesting to observe the forms in which Clough expresses ideas which are parallel to Goethe's ideas, and no doubt partly refinements of them. For instance, Dipsychus reflects in the course of one of his longest speeches :

> " What we call sin
> I could believe a painful opening out
> Of paths for ampler virtue. The bare field,
> Scant with lean ears of harvest, long had mocked
> The vext laborious farmer ; came at length
> The deep plough in the lazy undersoil
> Down-driving ; with a cry earth's fibres crack,
> And a few months, and lo ! the golden leas,
> And autumn's crowded shocks and loaded wains.
> Let us look back on life ; was any change,
> Any now blest expansion, but at first
> A pang, remorse-like, shot to the inmost seats
> Of moral being ? "

This is obviously an expansion, or a contraction, of Mephistopheles' description of himself as :

> " Ein Teil von jener Kraft,
> Die stets das Böse will, und stets das Gute schafft."

Goethe's words give a clear-cut idea of Natural Instinct driving violently against the beneficent power of Reason, and throwing it back, and so providing it with ever new occasions for triumphant progress. But Clough's figure of the plough in the undersoil is far from showing any understanding of the workings and uses of sin.   For there is nothing evil in what a plough intends, nor in what it is.   Sin is really the soil, with Clough, instead of the plough—the lazy subsoil that is reluctant to be of service.   It is not a force, it is the absence of force.   He develops this notion in the lines that follow the passage just quoted :

> " To leave the habitual and the old, and quit
>   The easy-chair of use and wont, seems crime
>   To the weak soul, forgetful how at first
>   Sitting down seemed so too."

It is Dipsychus himself that must represent sin so conceived, while the Spirit stands for the opposite principle of good.   There is a muddle here, not incapable of being removed ; but Clough failed to remove it.   His reason is on the side of the Spirit and his temperament on the side of Dipsychus ; and so he befriends Dipsychus while bringing him to defeat, and slurs the Spirit while he is according him victory. He protects his inconsistency by refusing to distinguish his rival forces specifically as the Good and the Bad—which is an unfortunate refusal to make in the writing of a moral poem.

Clough's idea of sin lacks boldness and definition when compared with Goethe's because Clough's sins had never been bold and definite. He had quelled his own instincts too early and too successfully to know much about passion. And with the force of passion there had atrophied in him the force of aspiration. Virtue had become negative and Puritan. Having shunned the lower rungs of the Platonic ladder of admirations, he had no way of rising again to the higher stages of the ascent, once he had descended from them in abandoning the god of his youth. He does not attempt to supply in his poem anything corresponding to Goethe's "das Ewigweibliche." The unhappy Dipsychus is cut off from the possiblity, of being helped up and on by any powerful force of attraction. He cannot rise by thinking of a goal to be won : if he is to rise at all it must be by painful deliberation on the process itself—by sheer tugging at his own boot-straps. By such a representation, instead of "clothing our modern existence with poetry," as Emerson says Goethe did, Clough deprived existence of the principal rag of poetry that properly belongs to it.

A true poet ought to find life beautiful anywhere ; and Clough does not find life beautiful in Venice ! Is there any excuse for the poem, then ? Is there an excuse for any work of art which concerns itself not with the beautiful, but only with the doubtful, and the despairing, and the negative ? Any answer to these questions but a flat No must seek to point out beauty under very effective masks. The beauty of *Dipsychus* is dressed in the grimmest of guises :

it inheres in the honesty and the courage of an unimaginative and an unswerving self-examination. It has been called the saddest poem ever written. If it is terribly sad to see a man hunt to the depths of himself and find so little to satisfy him, it is at least cheering to see him make the search, for once, and survive his disappointment—and even write rather gaily about it. Yet it is not to be denied that *Dipsychus* has the effect of a poem of despair.

To compare it with another English poem of despair, of the immediately preceding generation, is not merely to illustrate a change of fashions in the way of despair, but to show alongside of a denied despair which is depressing a professed despair which is positively exhilarating. Manfred is sick of life to the point of attempting suicide, and he finally dies hating and reviling all men and all spirits good and bad. But he does not actually commit suicide, and his revilings somehow show him endowed with enormous zest for human life and the contemplation of superhuman spirits. If any protagonist of Clough's had ever thought seriously of suicide, his stern creator would have compelled him to go through with it ; and furthermore Clough himself would have felt duty bound to commit suicide as soon as he had finished working out to this conclusion the problem of his puppet. Anything else he would have thought dishonest. This advantage in honesty that Clough's work has over Byron's is obvious from start to finish of the two works. And Clough has an equally unquestionable superiority in soundness and depth of thought. From the level of Clough's thinking, Manfred's pride in his guilt and his valour in the presence of threatening spooks are absurd. In this sense Clough is far above assuming to crush a mighty Demon with such words as :

> " I have not been thy dupe, nor am thy prey—
> But was my own destroyer, and will be
> My own hereafter. Back, ye baffled fiends !
> The hand of death is on me—but not yours ! "

Yet a majority of readers professing to esteem intelligence and honesty as " the two noblest of things " will agree that Byron is greater than Clough and writes about despair much more arrestingly. For what matters ultimately is that Byron has more passion than Clough and more energy. And in passion and energy—no matter how unseeing and misguided and marked for death—is hope, and strength and sense ; but sluggishness, and the necessity for forcing an interest in the world, no matter how honest and intelligent they may be, are a distinctly inferior sort of thing. In a universe which is movement, Byron and Manfred, who move, are greater than Clough and Dipsychus, who do not, and the age of Byron in literature greater than the age of Clough

Much of the sadness of *Dipsychus* proceeds from the disproof it affords of the Proverb: " He that ruleth his spirit is better than he that taketh a city.' For the meaning of that verse, to anybody who has been attracted by it in modern times, is that having

K

once ruled himself a man may go on confidently
to the taking of a city. But Dipsychus, like Clough,
has ruled himself and is unable to conquer a village
or even a good job, let alone a city. It is the man
of the Middle Ages to whom that situation is satisfactory. Surely the moderns are right in thinking
that unless a man arrives at the taking of his city—
that is, gets something done in the world—there
is no particular point to his ruling himself. Than
such a man, he who has taken cities without having
ruled himself is much more admired. Manfred is a
good example of a hero of this class. He flatters
that one of the twin selves in which man naturally
takes much the more pride and joy—the self that
needs ruling, not the self that rules. This is the self
that yearns and imagines and initiates, and this is
the self that is the rightful source and subject of
poetry. The heroes it sets up may have great
imperfections, but the critical spirit which objects
to these imperfections in Manfred will still be human
enough not to find the congenially critical Dipsychus
preferable to him.

Greater than either of the half-way conquerors,
Dipsychus and Manfred, is Faust, who discovers
that " Geniessen macht gemein "—conquers himself
—and then goes on to do such serviceable things as
to make wheat-fields out of a swamp. Faust re-
cognises the test of social utility. But Clough had
not at the time he wrote *Dipsychus* got genuinely
into the way of looking at life as an affair between the

individual and society : his habit was too strong of seeing it as an affair between man and God. He had been very thoroughly taught that the end of man was to glorify God, and was at this time engaged in the process, to the last not completely successful, of persuading himself that the end of man is to cherish and quicken life. He was retarded in this transition by the powerful influence on him of Carlyle. Carlyle tells man to work in the world for the good of his soul, and for the good of Soul generally—of the Absolute. The last, of course, comes to the same selfish thing as the first, when one refuses, as Carlyle did, to recognize any particular piece of work doing or proposed in his own world as worth the expenditure of effort. Clough gets a little ahead of Carlyle on this point but he remains behind Goethe. It required immense vitality, in addition to clearness of vision, to see life as Goethe saw it : Clough lacked the necessary vitality. He caught the idea, and merely as idea, held it in an even truer form than Goethe held it in, because he knew what work was so much better than Goethe did. But he failed to surround it with feeling and will ; and the pragmatic idea is one that requires especially large elements of will and feeling. Great stocks of will and feeling were in Clough, but long and severe restraint had made it impossible to use them with any freedom. Particularly at the time he wrote *Dipsychus*, he was much in the condition of the athlete who is " muscle-bound."

Everybody agrees that Goethe was a pragmatist: or that pragmatism is at least as good a word as any other for his comprehensive philosophy. A French scholar, M. Edouard Guyot, has recently developed the idea that Clough was a pragmatist—though also a rationalist—and an important precursor of that way of thinking which its founders insist is so old that to talk about precursors of it, at any rate in modern times, is scarcely to the point.

For a poet to be regarded as showing pragmatic tendencies, M. Guyot says, it will be necessary, first, "that the idea of action should hold an important place in his work, and that toward it should converge more than one psychological conflict"; and second, "that this idea should have presented itself to the author at a time when he was seeking truth for its own sake, and that he should have accepted it, not because he was satisfied with it instinctively, not because of the positive advantages which are attached to it, but because it gives to his curiosity or to his uncertainty a satisfaction as clear, as complete, as that which a person of different temperament would derive from a solution based upon recognition of the absolute, upon a definitive and unbroken arrangement of the universe."

Of these two tests Clough certainly meets the first. But it is not a very significant test. It will establish, not so much whether a poet is a pragmatist, as whether he is in any degree either a philosopher or a moralist, and so given to the use of abstract terms.

For in any philosophy worthy of the name, and in any system of morals, " the idea of action will hold an important place." It is a thing man has to think about ; and the psychological conflicts of sage and clown alike converge toward it, and in fact never converge toward anything else. It holds an important place with Kant, and with all the post-Kantian idealists. By its other name, work, it holds a very important place with Carlyle, and few men are to be described as pragmatists less aptly than he. To work only for the mortification of the flesh and the enrichment of the soul, and meanwhile to consent to see as valuable in itself no single piece of work actually going forward in one's own world, is not in all respects a different thing from sitting graciously on spikes and calling oneself a Buddhist. It is a very different thing from pragmatism. If pragmatic is to mean anything specific it must surely be limited to a philosophy which gives action not an important, but the important place : to a philosophy which celebrates action not merely as the means, but also as the end. And by this more exciting test for pragmatism, Clough is very much less of a pragmatist.

M. Guyot finds that Clough successfully meets his second test also. The decision here may perhaps be taken to depend on what is meant by being satisfied with an idea. In the last years of his life, when, if ever, Clough was a pragmatist, he does indeed appear to have enjoyed a considerable measure of contentment. He went about his work, and he loved his wife and children ; and " to be happy at home," says Dr. Johnson, " is the ultimate result of all ambition." On the other hand, he did not in these years work with anything like the enthusiasm which he possessed in the days when he held a fixed belief in the Christian God. Something of this may be laid to increasing age—though Clough's age increased so little beyond forty. But whatever may be true in the case of any other kind of philosophy, to be really satisfied with a philosophy of action implies very much more than mere contentment with routine. It implies action that represents constant and eager effort. It implies an interest in the doings of the world which will necessitate a struggle, not inevitably selfish, to play as considerable a part in them as possible. It implies these things, in a sense, even for the professed philosopher, who has chosen speculation for his work in life. It implies them much more in the case of a man still young and still not irrevocably committed to any single kind of work. Satisfaction, with these implications, the years of Clough's life after he began talking so much about action can scarcely be said to exhibit at all remarkably. But to enlarge upon this point would be to anticipate a later chapter.

M. Guyot sees Clough's philosophy of action revealed in full in *Dipsychus*. At any rate *Dipsychus* is the most philosophical of the poems : *The Bothie* indicates, but does not attempt fully to reveal, a philosophy that is more confidently and more purely a philosophy of action. *Dipsychus* was the poet's professed effort to think through the relation between the soul and matter—not metaphysically, indeed, but morally. It attacks the question, whether it is well to try to expand and strengthen that relation —which is action. Goethe, in his try at the problem, makes Faust definitely successful in his struggles with the world. At the end of the poem the hero is triumphant. In what we have of *Dipsychus* either of two pauses may be accepted as the conclusion : the abrupt breaking-off of *Dipsychus Continued*, or, eliminating that distinctly inferior sequel, the concluding scene of Part II of the poem itself. The opening lines of *Dipsychus Continued* are in key with what follows them, and they are not suggestive of triumph. Says Dipsychus, alone in his study:

> " O God ! O God ! and must I still go on
> Doing this work—I know not, hell's or Thine ! "

Clough was not a pragmatist, nor fractionally a pragmatist, when he wrote this as the serious exclamation of a Lord Chief Justice of England not definitely intended as either villain or fool. It is only fair to Clough to accept the earlier stopping-point. To do this is a kindness more to his reputation as artist than to his reputation as philosopher. For it is substituting an inconclusive for a conclusive ending. It is substituting for a conclusion definitely against a philosophy of action, one that accepts such a philosophy only bitterly and hopelessly, in despair of keeping hold of any other. No more in the life of his hero than in his own life does Clough show the philosophy of action leading to happiness, to security, or to real accomplishment.

Dipsychus is Clough's best poem, from the point of view of the student of him, for the very reason that it shows Clough at his weakest. At other times he is writing guardedly as the man he wills himself to be ; now press of circumstances has broken down the guard, and the undermost Clough, the temperament of the man, speaks out. It speaks out, not indeed as the whole man, but at least as more than half of him. And this temperament is unalterably opposed to a pragmatic way of taking things. It has spent so great and so dear a part of its life in revering the very highest things that it cannot be brought to revere things around. Thinking that action is the vital concern, willing frantically to become a man of action, does not avail. The tender conscience perseveres in looking inward and upward, and refuses to look round about. This is a principal reason why *Dipsychus* is so sad a poem. A man who has always managed himself well and bravely tries to command one last great improvement in himself, and his command is not obeyed. He tries to carry off the failure jauntily, by assuming that it is rather a success. But he fails to convince himself, as, with a few exceptions, he fails to convince the readers of his poem.

What might have enabled Clough to become a

true pragmatist was a firm belief in some theory of evolution. Goethe had such a belief. Carlyle had none, and lived the less happily for the want of it. Germs of such a theory may be found in *The Bothie ;* but Clough failed to cherish them. He had no training in science, and little that was scientific in his habit of mind. There is nothing to show it ever occurred to him that hope could come from this source. If he read the great books that paved the way for Darwin, he never speaks of them. Native individualism, training, association, chance, prevented him from gaining friendly acquaintance with the historical way of taking the world ; and so his immensely reverent spirit missed its chance of attaching itself to the only ideal that could have been an adequate substitute for the God of his youth. To believe in action, and neither in a clearly conceived God nor in Evolution is to try to live by bread alone. " What system of philosophy you hold," says Fichte, " depends wholly upon what manner of man you are." And Clough was the kind of man who cannot live by bread alone. The idea that so to live might, however, be the secret of living introduced into the latter part of his life a more deadly discord, though he kept it suppressed, than any of the uncertainties of his Oxford days.

The upshot of Clough's philosophizing, then, was only destructive. *Dipsychus* was an unintentional warning to its readers against a too complete adherence to the doctrines of Carlyle. Had it appeared in the year of its composition, it would probably have made much more stir than it created when it finally appeared, a decade after *The Origin of Species*. It would have met a very violent opposition, and it would have represented fairly well the state of mind of persons critical of the teachings of the Church, and would have prepared them to welcome the ideas of Darwin and Spencer and Comte. Published at the end of the 'sixties it served no such purpose. It was doomed then to unpopularity with both parties: for the heretical were strong now in the possession of a new science and of a new religion, the "Religion of Humanity," and could not be greatly pleased with a poem which expressed only the more negative of their opinions, and expressed even these, not ringingly, but bitterly and despairingly.

CHAPTER VIII

LAST YEARS

CLOUGH spent three years at his teaching in London. The first of them, it was remarked in the preceding chapter, he called at a later period the worst year of his life. But the two years that followed it were not much better. It began to appear to him that he had made a mistake in leaving Oxford. " I have jumped over a ditch for the sake of the experiment," he writes, " and would not be disinclined to be once again in a highway with my brethren and companions." The men his work in London brought him into contact with, under-graduates and seniors alike, were less congenial than the men he had known at Oxford. This may have been a matter more of his own increasing reserve than of an essential difference in quality between the two communities : he announces his unfortunate belief in the theory that a man can scarcely expect to make a new friend after he is thirty. His experience had been such as to make him especially dependent on friendships. He had had many dear friends, and the conditions of life in college had made it easy for him to see much more of them than it is possible for a man to see of his friends under usual circumstances. Now these old friends were scattering about the world, and marrying, and he missed them. And he had lost some of them, by leaving Oxford and the Church. Of new ones to fill these places there were, prominently, the Carlyles. He was a frequent visitor, in these years, at the house in Cheyne Row. He was the sort of man one would expect Carlyle to like : aside from his personal qualities, he was singularly free from associations, social or political or religious, with people and with things that Carlyle hated, and he must have been one of the most patient and unself-assertive of disciples. And Carlyle *did* like him. He says in a letter to Froude, after Clough's death : " A mind more vivid, more ingenious, more veracious, mildly radiant, I have seldom met with, and in a character so honest, modest, kindly. I expected great things of him."

The word that is surprising in this tribute is " ingenious." An ingenious man would have got more satisfaction out of living than Clough was getting at this time ; an ingenious man might even have made a success out of the University Hall experiment, which in Clough's hands failed, so that he lost his place there. Or if that work was hopelessly disagreeable, he might have found a way to shorten the time he gave it, in order to devote himself to pleasanter tasks. But he himself probably con-

sidered that ingenuity bordered on trickery, and
trickery on dishonesty ; there is nothing to show
that he ever attempted to display it or to cultivate
it. So his moral instinct would let him regard it
as cheating to find any spare moments to apply
to any other work than that he was hired to do.
His apologists are at great pains to explain that his
mind, though powerful, had this remarkable peculiarity, that it "could not work unless under a
combination of favourable circumstances." The
equally interesting reflection occurs in the *Memoir*
that the prospect that any writing might be profitable
"seemed to make it impossible to him to write."
This is to be mystical about a matter that Clough
himself would probably have liked to see stated more
frankly : he had more plough-horse than Arab in
him, and drudged unnecessarily because he liked
to drudge. This comes out in letters, written while
he was translating Plutarch, which tell how greatly
he prefers the task of translating to that of writing
for the *North American Review*, or even that of writing verse. In his moralizings he talks more and
more about patience—not a good sign that the high
expectations of him early formed and still enter-
tained by a smaller number of friends were ever
going to be fulfilled.

This, of course, is to be rather hard on Clough.
But it cannot be overlooked that the spectacle he
affords in this most important period of his life is
very disappointing. It is irritating to see coming

to so little a character so carefully and honestly forged and a mind that had been so fortunate in its opportunities for contacts of the sort most likely to be helpful. It is irritating to see a man so indecisive—to find him writing to his correspondents things like this : " As for the objects of life, Heaven knows ! they differ with one's opportunities. (*a*) Work for others—political, mechanical, or as it may be. (*b*) Personal relations. (*c*) Making books, pictures, music, etc. (*d*) Living in one's shell. ' They also serve who only stand and wait.' I speak as a philosopher, otherwise fool." But this frame of mind in Clough was not permanent, and perhaps the best thing to do is to hurry through with the extent of time that it lasted. It was not Clough himself that brought it to an end, one regrets to say, so much as press of circumstances. After he had left University Hall, Clough stayed on in London for a time as Professor of English Language and Literature at University College, at a salary, he tells Emerson, of thirty pounds a year. To the meekness with which he endured this poverty one prefers the defiance of a Johnson or even the gay irresponsibility of a Goldsmith.

A new college was founded out in Australia, and Clough applied for the principalship. He came near enough to getting it to become engaged on the prospect—to Miss Blanche Smith, of Combe Hurst, Surrey. But another man got the appointment. He tried to get a place in the Education

Office. But his friends were Liberals, and just as it seemed their efforts might be going to succeed, the Liberals were thrown out of office. In this pass he looked to America. In June 1852 he wrote to his friend Emerson to learn if in his judgment there was a chance of earning a living " anywhere between the Atlantic and the Mississippi, by teaching Latin, Greek, or English." The good opinion of Clough which Emerson had formed on his visit to Oxford had been strengthened by a liking for *The Bothie*. In the *Journal*, for 1849, occurs this passage : " Clough's beautiful poem I read again last in the sitting-room. 'Tis a kind of new and better Carlyle : the Homeric iteration is one secret ; the truly modern question and modern treatment another ; and there is abundance of life and experience in it. Good passages are,the prayer to the sun and moon and hours to pass slowly over Philip and Elspie, and good youth in it, as Elizabeth Hoar says." It was a kindly and cheering reply, therefore, which Clough received from Emerson ; and though he could not " take the next ship," as he was urged to do, he sailed on the *Canada* from Liverpool to Boston on October 30, 1852.

He had as fellow passengers on this voyage Thackeray and James Russell Lowell. With Lowell he immediately struck up a warm and lasting friendship. He found in him another fervent admirer of *The Bothie*. In a letter to C. F. Briggs, the editor of *Putnam's Monthly*, Lowell says of Clough : " I wish to write a review of his *Bothie* to serve him in event of a new edition. It is one of the most charming books ever written—to my thinking, quite as much by itself as the *Vicar of Wakefield.*" In another letter to the same correspondent Lowell calls *The Bothie* "a rare and original poem. I do not know," he says, " a poem more impregnated with the nineteenth century, or fuller of tender force, and shy, delicate humour." With Thackeray, too, Clough was on very friendly terms, though they did not keep up the friendship—and it would have been very surprising if they had kept it up, being men so unlike. Clough was not, of course, a celebrity in a class with these two. But at dinner, the last day out, toasts were drunk, starting with Thackeray, and to Lowell as " the American poet"; and Lowell, in responding, Clough says, " proposed the English poet, me!—and all the people stared at this extraordinary piece of information." This was his first taste of the small, but delightfully refreshing cup of fame that was proffered to him in America.

Clough spent some of his time on this journey in writing lyrics. These were included in later editions of the poems as *Songs in Absence.* Most of them are addressed to the lady who became his wife. They are lacking in many of the traditional virtues of love poetry. Clough was no Romeo: he is not passionate, and he does not praise his mistress nor seek to please her by saying things

prettily. There is some fervour, but he does not
exaggerate it. It is to be hoped that he was definitely
underestimating his feelings in one of the poems.
He has been lamenting that friendships do not survive partings, and turns in the last stanza to say
this of a stronger form of attachment :

> " But love, the poets say, is blind ;
> So out of sight and out of mind
> Need not, nor will, *I think*, be true,
> My own and only love, of you."

It cannot even be said that this is simplicity of
the expensive sort. Yet there is, perhaps, some
poetry, and the ultimate guarantee of sincerity, in
the fact that a man brought up on Virgil and Horace
can express to his beloved such rudimentary sentiments in such rudimentary words.

His first few days in Boston Clough spent in company with Thackeray, who was being received cor-
dially but much less uproariously than Dickens had
been. Thackeray moved on to New York in a few
days, and left the remaining literary honours of the
season to be paid to Clough. Emerson and Lowell
and Longfellow and the Ticknors and the Nortons
dined him and took him about, and made him feel
more at home in a strange land than he had felt
for a long time in his own country. It was not a
great number of people who thus interested themselves in him, but those who did so were of all
Americans the best known in England and the most
to be desired as friends. " I am not *at all* a distin-

guished literary man in some eyes here, remember,"
Clough writes home. He entered into the sober
entertainments of his New England friends naturally, and with much of the impressiveness of reserve,
and increased the strength, if not greatly the extent,
of his popularity. There is, for instance, an evening
of theatricals at the Nortons', and Clough pleases
everybody with an epilogue that he writes. And
there is a supper with Lowell, at which Webster
and Dana tell stories, and Clough effaces himself
and plays the part of a good listener. Everywhere
people had read *The Bothie*, and would lay a copy
of it on the parlour table, where its author would
be pleased to see it. Men sought his opinions, and
pondered them. Nothing could have been more
wholesome for Clough than the kindliness of this
reception.

A week after his arrival he took lodgings in Cambridge, where he lived the whole of his short stay
in America. He got his first pupil almost immediately, in a six-foot, seventeen-year-old scion of
the Winthrop family. Clough taught him Greek
three hours a day. Soon there is another boy or
two, and then a little private class in Ethics. His
friends get some writing for him to do for *The North
American Review* and *Putnam's*. Presently he ar-
ranges with Little, Brown & Co. to revise the
Dryden translation of Plutarch's *Lives* for them.
This last work pleased him only too well; he devoted
time to it that he would better have spent on under-

takings that might lead to something. His sponsors
advised him that his best chance in America was
to start a school for boys, or perhaps for girls.
Clough, for a time at least, took kindly to the idea.
In his Oxford and especially his Rugby training,
and in his friendships with just those men whose
recommendations would most impress American
parents, he had exceptional advantages for such an
enterprise. But he let the opportunity go. His
ambition, which he declares has revived in the Boston air, had not revived sufficiently ; or he had
overestimated the willingness he protests to his
fiancée to :

> " Apply for service ; day by day
> Seek honest work for honest pay,
> Without a fear by any toil
> The over-cleanly hand to soil."

Also his first delight with America had moderated
to a point which permitted such perceptions as that
" people are cleverer, and know more over there,"
and that " this climate certainly is to my somewhat
rheumatic constitution rather trying." And Carlyle
kept on trying to get him a Government position,
and at last in the spring of 1853 was able to hold
out the definite offer of a place, though a humble
place, in the Education Office. And Miss Smith
advised return. On June 22 Clough, who was not
much given to complaining of such things as the
weather, objects to a temperature of ninety-four
degrees, and on the next day still more stoutly

to a sudden change which has given him a cold. Some days later he telegraphs for a berth, and sails from New York by the next boat.

In the course of his eight months in America Clough had done a considerable quantity of writing. Particularly, the only magazine articles he ever had printed were done at this time. He makes in *The North American* for July 1853 his only appearance in the character of critic. He reviews the poems of Alexander Smith and of Matthew Arnold. On Smith's *Life Drama* he has some good things to say, but says them very tentatively—and in connection with a dull poem. It is the everyday subject matter that he approves, and he goes on to develop rather eloquently his ideal of modern poetry. " Could not poetry," he asks, " attempt to convert into beauty and thankfulness, or at least into some form and shape, some feeling, at any rate, of content, the actual, palpable things with which our everyday life is concerned : introduce into business and weary task-work a character and a soul of purpose and reality ? . . . Might it not divinely condescend to all infirmities ; be in all points tempted as we are; exclude nothing, least of all guilt and distress, from its wide fraternization ; not content itself merely with talking of what may be better elsewhere, but seek also to deal with what is here ? " The trouble with this description of the right poetry—there is more of it, but to the same effect—is that it makes no provisions, and seems not to feel the need of a pro-

vision, for poetry's remaining poetry while it does
all these things. One fears that Clough would have
admitted all knowledge as poetry, without insist-
ing on any evidences of the breath and finer spirit.
He finds his friend Arnold a better poet than Smith,
though he berates him, it is amusing to see, for
his share in " something of an over-educated weakness of purpose in Western Europe." He finds
in him " a disposition to press too far the finer
and subtler intellectual and moral susceptibilities."
Thus does the best of pots call the kettle black ;
and is justified in so doing, too, when it has contracted to tell what it honestly thinks of the kettle,
and when its first attention goes naturally to black-
ness, from having had sad experience of its own
with that phenomenon. The real fault, or the
main fault, of the essay is that it is too heavy-
handed.

This fault appears more glaringly in two attempts
at the light essay, which Clough published in *Putnam's* in the summer of 1853, under the title " Letters
of Parepidemus "—letters of a sojourner. Both are
oracular in style, and somehow desperately moral,
though not on moral subjects. The first is on
the necessity of unlearning, and is itself very didactic. The second is about hexameters : it argues
against them, and denies, what Arnold was later
to contend, that Homer can be translated successfully and to best advantage in hexameters. The
papers are sound enough, but in reading them one

longs for a touch of verve, and to secure it would welcome wild extravagance of opinion and shocking immorality. In addition to the intimate and the critical, Clough turned his hand to the political essay : this in a review of a work on social theories of the age. He has occasion here to be dubious of the advantages of liberty, and certain of what Carlyle and Ruskin had been telling people about the greater importance of service willingly rendered. The turn of his own that he gives to their teaching does not improve it : " It is very fine, perhaps not very difficult, to do every now and then some noble or generous act. But what is wanted of us is to do no wrong ones." To say things like that is to be, in all the length and breadth of the word, infelicitous.

At the same time that he was ruining his writing for publication with such early Puritan precepts as this, Clough was saying things in his letters that anticipate William James. Speaking of what he calls mysticism (he defines it as " letting feelings run on without thinking of the reality of their object "), he writes: " It won't do : twice two are four, all the world over, and there's no harm in its being so ; 'tisn't the devil's doing that it is ; *il faut s'y soumettre*, and all right." And again : " The plain rule in all matters is, not to think what you are thinking about the question, but to look straight out at the things and let them affect you ; otherwise, how can you judge at all ? " If

Clough could have seen it as at least as important that you should affect things as that things should affect you, and could have seen the two things at the same time—he might then have been the leader of desolate Carlyleans that Emerson hoped he would be. But he never got his glimpses of the truth properly co-ordinated. His American experience did, however, give him a somewhat more cheerful and more practical attitude toward the conduct of his own life.

Clough was not the man to think he had learned all about America in eight months, and did not write a book about his visit. All his casual remarks about American people and conditions show an open-mindedness and an utter freedom from prejudice that seem normal now, but were highly exceptional in the middle of the last century. He was willing from the first to find America as good a land as the mother country, and finished by liking it better. In making his comparisons he was struck by resemblances more than by differences, and so was able to please his Cambridge neighbours by telling them that he felt himself back in Oxford in living there. He was just the man to give the New Englanders full credit for their sincerity and their democratic kindliness, and to like them very little the less for their deficiency in cleverness and in *savoir-faire*. He is more disturbed by their superficiality : Emerson, he exclaims, is the only profound man in the country. The thing that pleased him most of all was the better position of the lower classes, and the practicability of being poor with as much decency and as much honour as the rich could enjoy. Such immediate and complete sympathy did not lead to the reception of impressions of the picturesque kind ; and Clough's book, if he had written it, would have been as much duller than Dickens', even to American readers, as it would have been fairer and more judicious.

A week after his return to England Clough took up his work in the Education Office—the work that was to occupy most of his time for the remaining eight years of his life. He had come to the Office late, and as rules of seniority governed promotion pretty completely there was little incentive to attempt to make a brilliant career for himself as a public servant. His letters do not complain of his work, as so many of Matthew Arnold's complain of similar tasks. He seems to have liked routine thoroughly. On June 12, 1854, he married Miss Smith, and in the autumn took a house in London, near Regent's Park. Here he lived for five years, and then removed to Campden Hill, in Kensington. The marriage was unquestionably a very happy one. It brought him more congenial friends than one, since his wife had a large and interesting family connection, which included the Nightingales. Three children were born to the Cloughs : two girls and a boy. Mrs. Clough, in the *Memoir*, says, what any one knowing him personally or through books

would know beforehand, that Clough was ideally
kind and attentive to his children, and loved nothing
more than to play with them. Lowell and other
men who saw in Clough the most indubitable genius
they had met made no mistake, perhaps, except in
the kind of genius they thought they saw. The
genius of an artist he lacked. But he had a positive genius for being that no less delightful thing,
a good man.

To read Mrs. Clough's touching denial of the
judgment, commonly made then as later, that
this life of her husband's was "a broken life," is
to be convinced by it. He had attained, she is
sure, a remarkable degree of peace. She explains
his failure to give expression to this peace by its
being the result not of a sudden conversion, surprised
and proud and anxious to make itself known abroad,
but of the patient thinking of years. It did not
quite recognize itself, that is ; and if it had done
so perhaps it would have been the less peace. There
is certainly a paradox in refusing to concede that a
man is at peace unless he is spending his days and
his energies in proclaiming it through the land :
to do so would be to introduce the singular dicho-
tomy, passive peace and active peace. His widow
says that Clough's peace was a "temper of mind" ;
and that suggests the making of the old distinction
between a temperamental and a reasoned attitude.
His spirit found peace when his mind discovered
that for mind there never is peace. Attending to

his intellectal history, we conclude, most rationally, that nothing but unrest was possible for him, because he had staked everything on finding truth and had failed to find it. We decide that he must have been unhappy. And then we are confronted by the facts—that he went about his work, in these later years, not gloriously, but steadily and comfortably and happily. And Mrs. Clough's words on the point have the ring of candour in them, something of the complete candour of her husband. If she could not read his mind, neither, certainly, can we.

Clough kept up correspondence with C. E. Norton, Lowell, Emerson, and Professor Child, supplying them the London gossip in politics and literature, and saying nothing about religion. Nor, in the letters that are printed, is there any discussion of the more substantial thinking of this important decade in the fields of science and economics and philosophy. He mentions Mill's *Dissertations* once, without a word to indicate that he has read them. That he saw something of the Arnolds we know from them, and he retained some intimacy with Carlyle. A new friendship that meant much to him was with Miss Florence Nightingale, who was a " double cousin " of his wife. He found in her a spirit very like his own, and endowed with a somewhat stronger vitality. She too had come through harrowing religious struggles to a philosophy of service. Sir Edward Cook speaks of the long talks they enjoyed having, at her house at Matlock, or in London. One of the reasons assigned for Clough's decline in health is that he over-exerted himself in devoting his spare time to her enterprise in the Crimean War. This, his wife says, was his favourite work ; and she considers that nothing gave him greater satisfaction than the large share he enjoyed of Miss Nightingale's trust and reliance.

It was for some reason a settled principle with Clough, after his undergraduate days, that he could write verse only in vacations and on journeys. But vacations from the Education Office were short, and devoted to his family. There was a three months' tour in Europe in 1856 to investigate military schools ; but the work to be done was real, and allowed no time for versifying. *The Bothie* was revised, and *Amours de Voyage* prepared for publication, and year after year saw no new literary undertaking entered upon. Yet Clough was meditating all the time a renewal of his poetical work, and in a new manner. He had found a new master, or a new source of suggestion, in Crabbe. He writes to Professor Child in 1856, " I have been reading pretty nearly through Crabbe lately. . . . There is no one more purely English (in the Dutch manner), no one who better represents the general result through the country of the last century. His descriptions remind even me of things I used to see and hear of in my boyhood. And sometimes, though rarely, he has really the highest merit." The opportunity to turn this inspiration to account was slow in coming, but came at last when his health failed him in 1861, and he was forced to travel in Southern Europe, and rest. Then he started the collection of tales which he called *Mari Magno*, the last and in some respects the best of his works.

The prologue promises that these tales will be about love and marriage. To tell them a little company of travellers across the Atlantic is provided—the author, as a youth, and " an elder friend, " a young and successful New England writer, an English clergyman, a rising lawyer of thirty-three, the ship's mate. Love is the dominant theme except in one of the six tales, all that were completed. This one is the poorest of the lot, and, like Chaucer, Clough ascribes the telling of it to himself. Of the others, two are by the lawyer, two by the clergyman, and one by the mate. All of them were written while Clough was travelling in Greece, in France, and in Italy, in the last six months of his life. He was working on a draft of The Clergyman's Second Tale, the story of Christian, when he was on his deathbed, in Florence. Death came before he had reached the end of it, but later a finished version, one he had presumably thought not good enough, was found among his papers. It is only in the author's own story that any of the foreign atmosphere of the places of composition is utilized. The Mate's Tale, though it is English, is

concerned with types that Clough did not know
well ; and it is outlined rather thantold. The four
other stories are about people exactly like Clough
himself and his friends ; and they show such complete and such ripened reflection on the problems
they present as to leave no doubt that they are
based on situations in Clough's own life—or better,
perhaps, they represent his working out of situations that *almost* occurred in his life.

The most remarkable merit of these stories is
the wisdom with which the state of marriage is
regarded. They do not, like most Victorian stories,
over-emphasize the mystical or the sentimental
aspects of marriage. On the other hand, they are
not too matter of fact. Clough seems to hit very
close to the golden mean between the practical and
the romantic, between the physical and the spiritual.
His understanding of all motives concerned, and
his sympathies with them, seem complete. Particularly strong and sensible is the opening story,
of the young college fellow persuaded by a married
cousin, a little older, whom he has loved, to forsake
academic wisdom and solitude and to go out and
taste real life in making a living for a wife of his own.
In the preference here declared may be found the
key of Clough's life, if there is ever anything so
rational as a key of a life. The lesson is the old
one of *The Bothie*, but taught now with fuller understanding and more seriously and in plainer words.
In plainness of words, indeed, Clough goes even

beyond Crabbe. He had been reminded of the things of his youth, as he wrote to Professor Child ; and being so reminded of them, he wrote about them in a heightened—perhaps better, a lowered—form of Crabbe's manner. But if he is more austere with his words than Crabbe, he is less austere with his people. They believe in happiness, all of them —in a stern way, are optimists. They get on their feet in life without trampling others. Like *The Bothie, Mari Magno* contains the kind of experience one would like to see added, in the way reading adds to the experience of young people, to the experience of students in the schools.

Mrs. Clough recounts fully, in the *Memoir*, the circumstances of her husband's declining health and death. He had never, she thinks, been particularly rugged, and the worry and strain of earlier years had told on his constitution. In 1859 he began to suffer from a succession of minor illnesses. His vacation in the fall of 1860 left him feeling unfit for work, and he secured a six months' leave of absence from the Education Office. He went first to Malvern, and then to the Isle of Wight. There he lived near Freshwater, and saw much of the Tennysons. In April of 1861 he set off alone for Constantinople and Greece, and wrote very cheerful letters back about the things he saw and the people he met. He tired of solitude, however, and returned to England in June, earlier than he had been expected. In July he went, again

it was the sanction of a superlatively honest man. He had sacrificed many things in order to be honest —had indeed made himself a specialist just in intellectual honesty. His speciality did not win him wealth nor much fame, but it won him the thoughtful attention and the respect of a limited number of men whose respect and attention were cautiously bestowed.

Some of the eulogies he won are from the men of all others of his age whose good opinion was most to be prized. In his own country Carlyle and Bagehot and Arnold praised him, and in America, Lowell and Longfellow and Emerson. Lowell has no doubt that he is a man of genius, as well as a man of the highest type of character. Longfellow says, simply : " I like him exceedingly ; with his gentleness, and his bewildered look, and his half-closed eyes." Emerson sees in him " a new and better Carlyle," and is so convinced of his strength and of the sureness of his insight that he appoints him " Bishop of all England," to gather up the wanderers Carlyle had left in the desert, and to lead them into the promised land. Carlyle himself, as we have seen, valued no less highly the man thus authoritatively singled out to undo his work, though he was unfortunate in his choice of words to express his appreciation. Bagehot awards Clough just the praise he would have liked best in thus refusing him praise : " He could not have borne to have his poems reviewed with ' nice remarks ' and senti-

mental epithets of insincere praise. He was equal
to his own precept :

" ' Where are the great, whom thou would'st wish to praise thee ?
Where are the pure, whom thou would'st choose to love thee ?
Where are the brave, to stand supreme above thee,
Whose high commands would cheer, whose chidings raise thee ?
 Seek, seeker, in thyself ; submit to find
 In the stones, bread, and life in the blank mind.'

To offer petty praise and posthumous compliments
to a stoic of this temper is like bringing sugar-plums
for St. Simeon Stylites."

It was Matthew Arnold who knew Clough best,
and who, in *Thyrsis*, did more than any other
man has done to perpetuate his memory. *Thyrsis*,
of course, does not really say much about Clough
—less even than *Lycidas* says about Edward King.
It says most about Arnold himself, and next most
about the Cumner hills, and about a favourite
poem of Arnold's own composition ; and it is rather
hard to see, what Arnold himself was only half
certain of, that in talking about these interesting
subjects he was really talking about Clough all the
time. And Arnold admits, in reply to an objection
of Principal Shairp's, that it was only one side, and
a less important side, of Clough that he had in mind.
" There is much in Clough," he concedes, " (the
whole prophet side, in fact) which one cannot deal
with in this way, and one has the feeling, if one
reads the poem as a memorial poem, that not enough
is said about Clough in it ; I feel this so much that
I do not send the poem to Mrs. Clough. Still

Clough *had* this idyllic side, too ; to deal with this suited my desire to deal again with that Cumner country : anyway, only so could I treat the matter this time." Arnold recognized that the real reason he wrote the poem was to follow up his earlier success with *The Scholar-Gypsy*. From the way in which he says "*if* one reads the poem as a memorial poem " it is fair to conclude that he expected one would read it as some other kind of poem. Yet he had specifically called *Thyrsis,* in a sub-title, " A Monody to commemorate the author's friend, Arthur Hugh Clough, who died at Florence, 1861." It is not meant to suggest that there is anything discreditable in this. It simply shows a wholesomely greater interest in a live oneself than in a dead somebody else, along with a desire to do the handsome thing by that somebody. And *Thyrsis* did do Clough's reputation a service. It is doing well by a man even to mention him in so good a poem. But some people's ideas of Clough are based on *Thyrsis*, and therefore probably come pretty far short of correspondence with reality.

But at other times, and for other purposes, Arnold said some very true things about Clough, and some splendid things. Everybody knows the eloquent peroration of the last of the *Lectures on Translating Homer*, with its selection of Clough as the shining instance of Homeric simplicity in writing and in living. At the start of his paragraph, Arnold declares his intention to speak of literary,

and not of general qualities of Clough's.   But he
gets to talking of the man himself, after a sentence
or two, as every one else has done who has set out
to talk of Clough's writings.   Three sentences are
especially good : " In the Saturnalia of ignoble
personal passions, of which the struggle for literary
success, in old and crowded communities, offers
so sad a spectacle, he never mingled.   He had not
yet traduced his friends, nor praised what he de-
spised.   Those who knew him well had the conviction that, even with time, these literary arts would
never be his."   Only the remark which introduces
this high tribute is misleading.   Arnold says : " His
interest was in literature itself ; and it was this that
gave so rare a stamp to his character."   Into conflict
with this comes the statement attributed to Vis-
count Morley, that he thought a Life of Clough ought
not to be included in the *English Men of Letters*
series for the reason that he was not primarily a
literary man.   And most people perhaps will find
it hard to believe, or to think Arnold actually believed, that the quality of Clough's interest in
literature was the deepest thing in him, the thing
that determined his character.   This deepest thing
was rather that his interest was in righteous living
itself.   But it is certainly true that he was not
interested in literature for the money and the
admiration he might be able to make it bring him.
If he had been so interested in it, he would doubtless have lived worse and written better.

The strength of Arnold's feeling for Clough is best shown in his letters. He writes to his much-loved sister, Mrs. Forster, in August of 1859 : " You and Clough are, I believe, the two people I in my heart care most to please by what I write." And after he has received the news of Clough's death, he writes to his mother : " That is a loss which I shall feel more and more as time goes on, for he is one of the few people who ever made a deep impression upon me, and as time goes on, and one finds no one else who makes such an impression, one's feeling about those who did make it gets to be something more and more distinct and unique. Besides, the object of it no longer survives to wear it out himself by becoming ordinary and different from what he was. People were beginning to say about Clough that he never would do anything now, and, in short, to pass him over. I foresee that there will now be a change, and attention will be fixed on what there was of extraordinary promise and interest in him when young, and of unique and imposing even as he grew older without fulfilling people's expectation."

There is a special interest in Arnold's comment on Clough in that it is the voice of a poet who did a great work in the world, concerning another poet, remarkably like himself in nature and in training, who did very much less. The two are generally discussed together in reviews of nineteenth-century literature and entitled " The Poets of Doubt." A symmetrical way of correlating the title and the difference in accomplishment is to say that the doubt overcame the one poet and was overcome by the other ; and there is something besides symmetry to justify the statement. Yet the prevailing tone of the poetry of the comparative failure is never complete despair, and is usually courage and hope. This contrast might be taken as material for a study in the effects of repression. The young Arnold, when he experienced despair, bayed the moon right humanly and lugubriously, and by so doing relieved his chest and his nerve centres of a highly unprofitable kind of emotion. Whereas Clough, when he despaired, remembered too scrupulously, what he and Arnold had both been carefully taught, that despair is unmanly, and so set to work to sing, as lustily as he could—which was not very lustily— that God, if not indeed in his heaven, was yet doubtless somewhere about ; and strained his voice by this feat of ventriloquism.

It is agreeable to see that Arnold still finds his old friend " imposing " in his later years, and not merely disappointing. He did not feel that the contradiction of expectation by fulfilment was particularly violent, and did not try to explain it. A number of reasons for it have been assigned by other commentators : that Clough's habit of mind was too critical, that he was too fully engrossed with his ideas, that he was too negligent of the conventions of writing, that he was too indecisive, that he was not sensitive enough to beauty. All this is a destructive sort of criticism ; but the kind of analysis that leads to it is tempting. It is the contradictions a man's life affords that arrest attention ; and this difference between what his youth promised and what his maturity fulfilled is one of a number of marked contradictions which the life of Clough presents. The first of these, perhaps, is that contradictions should appear at all in a life so controlled and so balanced as Clough's.

" The dangerous edge of things, " says Browning, is what interests us ; and Clough was a seeker after peace, and steered away from dangerous edges. But in avoiding some, he came upon others—or rifts appeared, in what had seemed to be safe ground. He was an especially religious man, and as a result acted and talked so as to get himself known as particularly irreligious. By Spartan methods he developed and retained a power of will, a superiority to temptation, which amazed the men who knew him ; yet his name has been in danger of becoming a byword for irresolution. He was a man of intelligence and yet set up as a poet without any real appreciation of the first principles of versification. These are a few of the major contortions in what is at first sight the unpromisingly straight and smooth record of Arthur Hugh Clough.

There are three ways of explaining these contradictions—that is, of saying something more about them than that they exist. They may be discussed, first, as the coming together in the individual, considered as an arena, of two opposing tendencies of his age. Or, second, regarding the individual as responsible, and not merely as a battleground, a pair of conflicting traits can be found in his character to correspond to and to provide a foundation for each specific contradiction. Or, third, still resting responsibility mainly on the man, there may be discovered in him some one fatal cleft, so far down in the roots of his nature as to have introduced division into all his counsels and all his sentiments. Attacks of all three kinds have been plentifully directed at the joints in the armour of Clough.

Proceeding on the first of these methods, that of explaining a man in terms of universal, or at least of national, chronology, some critics have seen in Clough a man of the seventeenth century living among Early Victorians, while others have hailed him as a citizen of our own present day living among Early Victorians. Others still have pronounced him Early Victorian of the Early Victorians ; but practically all of these have gone on to say, or to imply, that the persistent quality which establishes the first two decades of the reign of Victoria as a particular and a definite age is just that in that time there was not one age going forward but two ages, two remote ages, both of them struggling and crowding into the one limited series of calendar years. So that Clough is still a man of two ages, and for the very reason that he is the quintessence of one age. He is a dual personality in a time when everything is dual. He is a doubter in an Age of Doubt.

Assuming that the logic of this is unimpeachable, which it probably is not—but assuming it, it remains to ask first, if any age that ever has amounted to anything has not been an age of doubt, and, second, if the Early Victorian period specifically was not much more an age of cocksureness than of doubt. Macaulay and Dickens were its two most effective voices, and who was ever more cocksure than either of them? Nor were Carlyle and Mill devoid of strong convictions and the courage of them. So rank did cocksureness grow, and so completely did it overspread the land, that in the next generation Matthew Arnold, with the general agreement of the intelligent, was to pronounce the English just the smuggest and most self-satisfied race of all the races of the Western world, and their cocksureness, their perfect peace of mind, to be the greatest of all their faults. Few times and places have presented a busier spectacle of people unreflectively getting things done than the middle of the nineteenth century in England. Doubters were so rare that they amazed themselves and others, and were talked about. People who are particularly interested in them, who find them "significant," can call the period an age of doubt. For the same reason they could call the middle of the eleventh century an age of doubt.

It is possible to look at any large community

of recent times as divided into two parts—the few more thoughtful, and the many less thoughtful, and to describe the difference between the two sections as a difference of time : the intelligent are separated from the less intelligent by years or by centuries. Are these, then, to be regarded as ahead of their time, or are those to be described as behind it ? Are these advanced, or are those backward ? And when Tolstoi deliberately drops out of the presumed van of civilization and incorporates himself as completely as he is able with the rear, are we to call him a leader or a straggler ? Is our time scheme to rest on realities or on ideals ? Is the Early Victorian temper the dyspeptic temper of Carlyle, who hated Early Victorian England, or the unruffled temper of Macaulay, who loved it ? Was William Morris more of his age when he was longingly averting his gaze from his age to the past, or when he was longingly averting his gaze from his age to the future ? Our contemporary Mr. Wells writes fantastic stories about the twenty-fifth and thirtieth centuries A.D. Is he ahead of his time in so doing, or of it because he is interested in working out problems he sees about him, or behind it because he writes that most primitive of things, the fairy tale ?

These questions are put as tending to show once more how difficult is the task of determining the relation of a man to his time. It is particularly difficult in the case of a man of the nineteenth century—or in the case of a man of our own century. Earlier ages had discerned that they rested on the shoulders of the ages that preceded them ; but the nineteenth century was the first to set deliberately about taking advantage of all the privileges of the position. Men took to skipping from one pair of antecedent shoulders to another, and pausing a longer or shorter time on some vantage point to proclaim its superiorities. Many a man found it desirable to spraddle, and stretched himself out with one foot, say, on Late Byzantium and the other on Early Judaea, his left hand on the French Revolution and his right on the Birth of Time. For him to turn from his religious to his political and then to his artistic ideas or his metaphysics was—to use a comparison fairly incompatible with the one which precedes—for him to roam up and down the centuries as an organist wanders over his stops. Under such circumstances it is necessary when one says that a man is consistently of the nineteenth century to say also in what narrow respect he is of the nineteenth century—and even then what one says is likely to have either no meaning at all, or one meaning for one man and another for another.

The respect in which Clough was most consistently of the nineteenth century is that all of the settings he uses are nineteenth-century settings. His long narrative poems are all of them about people of his own time ; and so are the stories that his lyrics suggest—for a lyric always suggests a story of some sort as its background. Tennyson and Browning and Arnold took much of their material, most of it, indeed, from the past, and often from the traditions of other nations than their own. But Clough's criticism of life is invariably of the life of Britons of his day and generation. This is a real peculiarity. Its importance is lessened, but by no means destroyed, by remembering what modern poems *Idylls of the King* and *Empedocles on Aetna* and *The Statue and the Bust* are, and how English, in spite of their foreign or antique subject matter. Clough found human life enough in the world about him without going far afield for it. His mind, indeed, however powerful, had not the intrepidity for travelling. It was still finding plenty to feed on in the home pasture when it ceased its activities.

It is not to be denied that the problems Clough worked at are also all of them nineteenth-century problems, though it might be urged that the nineteenth century made its own nearly all problems of all times. And it was the most universal and timeless of these problems that interested Clough. The nature of friendship and love and marriage and parenthood, the service of God and fellow service—he examines directly these large and eternal things, and not merely abnormal or unusual instances of them, or aspects of them considered to be new. He was not the man to care much whether his works were up-to-date or not and whether they were novel or not. Pettiness of all sorts, over-valuation of little things, was what he hated most, and he was singularly successful in avoiding it. Differentiating a vast number of aspects of a thing, and arranging them, perhaps chronologically, is the kind of thing he called "fiddle-faddling": just as the people who find profit and delight in that kind of juggling find "fiddle-faddling" Clough's disposition to sit for ever on large problems he could not solve instead of deserting them for little problems that he could solve. But others than philosophers of the pigeon-holing school may fairly object to this disposition of Clough's. And it is certainly a respect in which he was not typical of his age.

Archbishop Whateley said of Clough that he had no following : meaning, specifically, that his defection carried out of the Church no other men than himself. This is true, and may be taken as showing on Clough's part either sense and consideration or a lack of courage. To call his refusal to proselytize good sense is perhaps to be reminded of the great chapter in which Dean Swift so satisfactorily proves that all revolutions and discoveries in human thought are varieties of madness; and calling it lack of courage, one may remember Emerson's dictum that "there is a certain headiness in all action," and that courage is willingness to act. If Clough had been willing, early in his life, to set limits to his thinking, to pick a direction and a road and to keep the road and pay no attention to byways, however highly recommended—if he had been willing to do this, he might have added a new form of protest against the Church to the other fine enthusiasms of his day, and might have ridden off on it and cut a figure. But before he could mount for his ride and gallop off to become another Great Victorian, it was necessary that he should tell himself that he had settled problems which he felt that he had not settled, and this for better and for worse he was unable to do.

In a world in which the chances of a man's accomplishing anything memorable are small, it may appear graceless to be asking so insistently why this man did not accomplish more, instead of marvelling that he accomplished so much as he did. New, though perhaps small, editions of Clough have been appearing at rather short intervals ever since his death. He wrote and he is read. Public taste, on the whole, seems to be moving in his direction rather than away from him, so that he will probably continue to find readers. And so long as he finds them they will probably, even though they like him, keep on finding him something of a failure, and speculating on why he failed. Lack of determination, inadequate opportunity, limited comprehension—here are the causes of failure ; but Clough had a strong and steady will, the best of training and of friends, a wealth of good

sense. More careful examination will show, perhaps, that the determination was too content to
remain determination instead of removing the need
for itself, that the training, though splendid for the
usual boy, was of the wrong kind for at least one
boy, and that a disproportionate share of the good
sense rested on merely vicarious experience. But
behind these suppositions will lurk a presentiment
of some unescapable limitation in the man's physical
nature. He was not sufficiently sensuous. He
did the best he could with a nervous system that
was simply not finely enough organized, not delicate
enough, to delight and gloriously to succeed in
creative effort.

INDEX

Printed in Great Britain by Butler & Tanner, *Frome and London.*